MARION FOALE'S CLASSIC KNITWEAR

MARION FOALE'S CLASSIC KNITWEAR

A beautiful collection of 30 original patterns

MARION FOALE
Photography by Rick Best

Rodale Press, Emmaus, Pennsylvania

Author's note

The preparation of this book has involved a
great many people, and I should like to
acknowledge my grateful thanks to the
following: the ladies who knitted up all the
garments; Rick Best for the photography;
Carole White at Premier Model Agency;
Marylyn Larkin for styling the photographs;
Anne Matthews at Vogue for meticulously
checking each pattern; Marit Allen for
providing the captions to each garment;
and to Chris Jones for planning the
whole project and organizing us all.

MARION FOALE

Published by Rodale Books
Rodale Press Inc
33 East Minor Street
Emmaus, PA 18049

Library of Congress Cataloging in Publication Data

Foale, Marion.
Marion Foale's Classic Knitwear.

1. Knitting-Patterns. 2. Sweaters. 3. Vests.
I. Title II. Title: Classic Knitwear.
TT825.G63 1985   746.9'2   85-8203
ISBN 0-87857-583-9 hardcover
ISBN 0-87857-584-7 paperback

AN EDDISON·SADD EDITION

Edited, designed and produced by
Eddison/Sadd Editions Limited
2 Kendall Place, London W1H 3AH

Phototypeset by Bookworm Typesetting,
Manchester, England
Originated, printed and bound in The Netherlands
by Druckerij de Lange/Van Leer

THE PATTERNS

EMILY 10
Ladies Twenties-style wool jumper

MAUD 14
Lean, sophisticated waistcoat in the same mood

AGATHA 19
Ladies cardigan, the perfect match for Emily

SCHOOLDAYS 25
Long, tunic-line wool sweater

GAMES 27
Sports sweater for men and women

SWEAT SHIRT 31
Bright, chunky child's sweater in double knit wool

CLASSIC CARDIGAN 34
Traditional, essentially English ladies cardigan

CLASSIC JUMPER 39
Long- or short-sleeved, to twin with the Cardigan

TENNIS 42
Simple and sensible long wool cardigan

SQUASH 47
Extra long, fully fashioned ladies waistcoat

BETH 50
A 'school' sweater in thoroughbred style

ZIGGY 55
Sweater for teens and ladies in Guernsey style

SOCCER 58
Sturdy, sporty man's sweater in double knit wool

SOPHIE 62
Pretty jumper patterned with lacy, beaded flowers

OSCAR 66
Light-weight indoor cardigan for men

GEORGE 71
Aran-style slip-over for men and women

HOCKEY 74
Casual, extra-long sports sweater for ladies

LLOYD 77
Rugged pullover for country-loving men

DAISY 81
Smock-shaped sweater, sporty or pretty for girls

LILLIAN 84
Elegant ladies cardigan with 'polka dot' beads

DOROTHY 89
Beaded jumper to match Lillian

ROCKY 91
Thick cotton summer slip-over for men

BOSANOVA 94
Dramatic V-neck sweater for ladies

CLIFTON 97
Man's classic sweater in chunky cotton

BADMINTON 101
Slender and summery jumper for ladies

GRAMPA 105
Serenely simple ladies jumper in thick cotton

RUGGER 109
Two versions of a sporty sweater for men and women

CROQUET 115
Another long, summery jumper for ladies

SPRINT 119
Dainty ladies vest in fine cotton

DANNY 123
Casual, sporty man's sweater in thick cotton

INTRODUCTION

Marion Foale was one of the new wave of English designers to graduate from the Royal College of Art in London during the decade we now nostalgically think of as the 'Swinging Sixties'. Together with her partner, Sally Tuffin, she designed young, lively fashions that mirrored the mood of the time.

Today, Marion Foale is better known as a designer of knitwear in the classic mould with a devoted international following. Her designs are deceptively simple, relying on their immaculate shaping and the imaginative use of traditional stitches for their stylish good looks. Sleeves are knitted onto the body of the garment and shoulder seams knitted together to give the smooth, clean shape that is one of her hallmarks.

With a reputation for beautifully finished, expertly knitted garments, Marion's standards are high. Her team of knitters have to supply a tension square with every garment they knit and each finished piece is carefully inspected before being delivered to the customer. In her *Notes for the Knitter* opposite Marion describes the techniques she uses to achieve the perfect garment.

In their ready-made form her designs are to be found in discerning high fashion shops in America, Europe and the Far East at prices that inevitably put them beyond the reach of many of her admirers. So it is not surprising that when her designs are published in pattern form in magazines they prove immensely popular. *The Sunday Times* and *Vogue* have recorded thousands of requests from hand knitters for Marion Foale patterns.

Thirty of Marion's most popular designs are featured in MARION FOALE'S CLASSIC KNITWEAR. Each is an example of the timeless, easy styling that she has perfected.

There is a comprehensive range of waistcoats, jumpers, slip-overs, cardigans and sweaters for men, women and children. Some patterns are sized for both men and women and all patterns are designed in a wide size range.

Each design has been modelled for the book and the accompanying caption describes the garment in detail. The instructions appear alongside with charts where necessary. Here also another photograph shows the garment laid flat so that the knitter can clearly see the stitch pattern and construction. Abbreviations, a glossary of knitting terms, and a needle conversion chart are provided overleaf.

With this book any home knitter can now produce her own superb collection of Marion Foale knitwear at a fraction of its ready-made cost.

NOTES FOR THE KNITTER

One of the main styling features of these garments is that they are constructed in one piece with just the side and sleeve seams to sew through. I feel that this suits the style of my approach to knitwear design — it is relaxed and clean looking. It also does away with bulky shoulder seams and sleeves that don't set well into their armholes.

Please read the following tips before starting to knit. They are very important.

TENSION
Most sizing problems are due to inaccurate tension (gauge). It is **_absolutely essential_** that your tension is correct so please always knit a tension square before starting any of the designs. The correct tension for each garment is given in the instructions together with the finished measurements. If necessary, change to a larger or a smaller needle.

JOINING YARN
Never join yarn in the middle of a row. It always shows and can easily come apart. Instead, join yarn at the beginning of a row.

EDGES
Where possible, try to work a knit stitch as the first and last stitch of every row. This makes a neat, tidy edge with regular 'notches' that looks good and makes the sewing up of seams so much easier.

SHOULDER SEAMS
All the shoulder seams in this book are knitted together. The emphasis this gives is a feature of the design of each garment. The seams should be knitted neither too tightly nor too loosely, so that they 'give' with the rest of the knitting.

SIZES
The first size given is the smallest. Larger sizes are shown in brackets.

INSTRUCTIONS IN BRACKETS
Where instructions are shown in brackets they should be repeated by the number of times stated immediately after the bracket.

MAKING UP
When sewing up each garment it is best to use the yarn it was knitted in. Using a tapestry needle, oversew or flat stitch seams together wherever possible. If you have worked a knit stitch at either end of each row you will be able to sew the pieces together from 'notch' to 'notch' and the seam will lie flat and be almost invisible. If the garment is knitted in reverse stocking stitch or some similar pattern, or in cotton, back stitch must be used instead. Watch that you don't sew the seams too tightly. They should be as relaxed as the knitting. Make sure, too, that all ends of seams are very securely finished.

PRESSING
I always sew the garment completely together and then press on the wrong side of the work using a steam iron on the appropriate setting. Take great care not to over-press and avoid pressing the welt, cuffs and other ribbed parts. A good finish to a knitted garment makes it look professionally made.

WASHING
Follow the washing instructions on the ball band.

YARNS
No particular brand of yarn is recommended. The choice is left to you, but of course good quality, and therefore more expensive, yarns will give a better finished result.

COTTON
Cotton types are not so specifically defined as wool. Check the ball bands for recommended needle size and tension and choose accordingly. This book refers to two weights of wool and two of cotton. The fine-weight cotton is roughly equivalent to 4 ply wool and the thick-weight cotton to double knitting quality wool. Do be sure though that your tension is correct before you start to knit.

Happy knitting!

MARION FOALE

GLOSSARY
OF KNITTING TERMS

BRITISH	AMERICAN
50 gm	approx 1¾ ounces
cast off	bind off
cast off in rib	bind off in rib
reverse stocking stitch	reverse stockinette stitch
stocking stitch	stockinette stitch
tension	gauge
work straight	work even
yarn forward, yarn round needle	yarn over needle

ABBREVIATIONS

dec = decrease
g.st = garter stitch
inc = increase
k = knit
kb = knit through back of stitch
kss = knit slipped stitch from cable needle
p = purl
pb = purl through back of stitch
pss = purl slipped stitch
psso = pass slipped stitch over
rib = rib, ribbing
r.st.st = reverse stocking stitch

sl. = slip
sl.IB = slip one stitch onto a cable needle and leave at back of work
sl.IF = slip one stitch onto a cable needle and leave at front of work
s.st.h = spare stitch holder
st(s) = stitches
st.st = stocking stitch
tbl = through back of loop
tog = together
yfwd = yarn forward

KNITTING NEEDLE SIZE CONVERSION CHART

British Imperial	British Metric	Continental	American
14	2 mm	2 mm	0
13	2¼ mm	2½ mm	1
12	2¾ mm	2½ mm	1
11	3 mm	3 mm	2
10	3¼ mm	3½ mm	3
9	3¾ mm	3½ mm	4
8	4 mm	4 mm	5
7	4½ mm	4½ mm	6
6	5 mm	5 mm	7
5	5½ mm	5½ mm	8
4	6 mm	6 mm	9
3	6½ mm	6½ mm	10
2	7 mm	7 mm	10½
1	7½ mm	7½ mm	11
0	8 mm	8 mm	12
00	9 mm	9 mm	13
000	10 mm	10 mm	15

EMILY
Ladies jumper in 4 ply wool

A jumper with a hint of the Twenties both in its length and the stylish Art Deco influenced diamond and ladder pattern. The garter stitch ladders and two row moss stitch diamond pattern are worked on to a stocking stitch base, and lead to a neat preppy garter stitch collar set on a ribbed stand neck.

MATERIALS
10 (11: 11: 12) 50 gm balls 4 ply wool
2 2¾ mm (12) needles
2 3¼ mm (10) needles
4 2¾ mm (12) double pointed needles
stitch holders

MEASUREMENTS
Bust
86 (91: 97: 102) cm
34 (36: 38: 40) in
Actual measurement
98 (104: 109: 114) cm
38½ (41: 43: 45) in
Finished length to shoulder
71 (71: 71: 71) cm
28 (28: 28: 28) in
Sleeve length
52 (53: 54: 54) cm
20½ (21: 21½: 21½) in

TENSION
28 sts and 36 rows for a 10 cm (4 in) square worked in st.st on 3¼ mm (10) needles

BACK AND FRONT
Work both the same. With 2¾ mm (12) needles cast on 134 (142: 150: 158) sts. Work 9 cm (3½ in) in k2, p2 rib, inc 1 st extra at end of last row. (135: 143: 151: 159) sts. Change to 3¼ mm (10) and continue in st.st. Work 34 rows. Now work 1st part of pattern as follows:
With right side facing
1st row: k 67 (71: 75: 79) sts, p1, k to end of row.
2nd row: p 67 (71: 75: 79) sts, k1, p to end of row.

3rd row: k 66 (70: 74: 78) sts, p1, k1, p1, k to end of row.
4th row: p 66 (70: 74: 78) sts, k1, p1, k1, p to end of row.
5th row: k 65 (69: 73: 77) sts, (p1, k1) 3 times, k to end of row.
6th row: p 65 (69: 73: 77) sts, (k1, p1) 3 times, p to end of row.
These last 6 rows set pattern. Continue as set inc the diamond by 2 sts every k row. Work 20 rows in all. Now work diamond in reverse as follows:
21st row: k 59 (63: 67: 71) sts, (p1, k1) 9 times, k to end of row.
22nd row: p 59 (63: 67: 71) sts, (k1, p1) 9 times, p to end of row.
23rd row: k 60 (64: 68: 72) sts, (p1, k1) 8 times, k to end of row.
24th row: p 60 (64: 68: 72) sts, (k1, p1) 8 times, p to end of row.
These last 4 rows set the pattern. Continue as set dec the diamond by 2 sts every k row until the 38th row has been worked. These 38 rows make the first part of the pattern. Now work the 2nd part as follows:
1st row: with right side facing k 47 (51: 55: 59) sts, p1, k11, (p2, k3) 3 times, p2, k11, p1, k to end of row.
2nd row: p 47 (51: 55: 59) sts, k1, p39, k1, p to end of row.
3rd row: k 46 (50: 54: 58) sts, p1, k1, p1, k10, (p2, k3) 3 times, p2, k10, p1, k1, p1, k to end of row.
4th row: p 46 (50: 54: 58) sts, k1, p1, k1, p37, k1, p1, k1, p to end of row.
5th row: k 45 (49: 53: 57) sts, (p1, k1) 3 times, k8, (p2, k3) 3 times, p2, k9, (p1, k1) 3 times, k to

end of row.
6th row: p 45 (49: 53: 57) sts, (k1, p1) 3 times, p34, (k1, p1) 3 times, p to end of row.
These last 6 rows set the pattern. Continue as set inc the 2 diamonds by 2 sts every k row. Work 20 rows in all. Now work pattern in reverse as follows:
21st row: k 39 (43: 47: 51) sts, (p1, k1) 9 times, k2, (p2, k3) 3 times, p2, k3, (p1, k1) 9 times, k to end of row.
22nd row: p 39 (43: 47: 51) sts, (k1, p1) 9 times, p22, (k1, p1) 9 times, p to end of row.
23rd row: k 40 (44: 48: 52) sts, (p1, k1) 8 times, k3, (p2, k3) 3 times, p2, k4, (p1, k1) 8 times, k to end of row.
24th row: p 40 (44: 48: 52) sts, (k1, p1) 8 times, p 24, (k1, p1) 8 times, p to end of row.
These last 4 rows set the pattern. Continue as set dec the 2 diamonds by 2 sts every k row until the 38th row has been worked. These 38 rows make the 2nd part of the pattern. Now work the 3rd part as follows:
1st row: with right side facing k 39 (43: 47: 51) sts, (p2, k3) 11 times, p2, k to end of row.
2nd row: p.
Repeat these last 2 rows 11 more times.
Shape armholes
With right side facing and working in pattern k the first 9 sts and put these sts on a s.st.h, work to last 9 sts and put them on a s.st.h. Turn and continue on remaining 117 (125: 133: 141) sts. Now work 13 more rows in pattern. These last 38 rows make the 3rd part of the pattern. Now work 4th part of pattern as follows:
1st row: with right side facing k 18 (22: 26: 30) sts, p1, k11, (p2, k3) 11 times, p2, k11, p1, k to end of row.
2nd row: p 18 (22: 26: 30) sts, k1, p79, k1, p to end of row.
3rd row: k 17 (21: 25: 29) sts, p1, k1, p1, k10, (p2, k3) 11 times, p2, k10, p1, k1, p1, k to end of row.
4th row: p 17 (21: 25: 29) sts, k1, p1, k1, p77, k1, p1, k1, p to end of row.
5th row: k 16 (20: 24: 28) sts, (p1, k1) 3 times, k8, (p2, k3) 11 times, p2, k9, (p1, k1) 3 times, k to end of row.
6th row: p 16 (20: 24: 28) sts, (k1, p1) 3 times, p74, (k1, p1) 3 times, p to end of row.
These last 6 rows set the pattern. Continue as set inc the 2 diamonds by 2 sts every k row.

Work 20 rows in all. Now work the diamonds in reverse as follows:
21st row: k 10 (14: 18: 22) sts, (p1, k1) 9 times, k2, (p2, k3) 11 times, p2, k3, (p1, k1) 9 times, k to end of row.
22nd row: p 10 (14: 18: 22) sts, (k1, p1) 9 times, p62, (k1, p1) 9 times, p to end of row.
23rd row: k 11 (15: 19: 23) sts, (p1, k1) 8 times, k3, (p2, k3) 11 times, p2, k4, (p1, k1) 8 times, k to end of row.
24th row: p 11 (15: 19: 23) sts, (k1, p1) 8 times, p64, (k1, p1) 8 times, p to end of row.
These last 4 rows set the pattern. Continue as set dec the 2 diamonds by 2 sts every k row until the 38th row has been worked. These 38 rows make the 4th part of the pattern. Now work the 5th part as follows:
1st row: with right side facing k 10 (14: 18: 22) sts, (p2, k3) 20 times, k to end of row.
2nd row: p.
Repeat last 2 rows 18 more times. These 38 rows make the 5th part of the pattern. Leave all sts on a s.st.h for shoulder seams and collar.
Shoulder seam
Work 2 the same. With 3¼ mm (10) needles put 27 (31: 35: 39) sts from the back and the same from the front on to spare needles. Place these 2 needles side by side with the wrong sides of work facing each other. Then working on the right side of work, k tog a st from each needle to give 1 st on the right hand needle. *K tog the next 2 sts (now 2 sts on right hand needle) then pass the 1st of these 2 sts over the second. Repeat from * to work rest of sts.

COLLAR
With right side facing and 2¾ mm (12) needles put the sts for the neck plus 2 sts (one from each shoulder seam) on 3 of the needles allowing for collar opening at centre front. Work 10 rounds in k1, p1 rib. Now divide for collar and work in rows. At centre front turn and continue in g.st until collar measures 9 cm (3½ in) from pick up row. With wrong side of collar facing, cast off. (*Collar should be slightly held in with cast off row, not stretched or fluted or pulled in too tightly*).

SLEEVES
Work 2 the same. With 3¼ mm (10) needles and right side of work facing pick up and k 9 sts

from s.st.h (armhole shaping), 139 sts evenly along armhole edge with centre st at shoulder seam and 9 sts from s.st.h. (157 sts). Then dec 1 st at each end of every 4th row as follows: k2, sl.1, k1, psso, k to last 4 sts, k2 tog, k2 until 79 (77: 75: 75) sts remain.

Shape cuff

With wrong side facing dec 27 (21: 15: 11) sts evenly across row. (52: 56: 60: 64) sts. Change to 2¾ mm (12) needles and work 9 cm (3½ in) in k2, p2 rib. Cast off loosely in rib.

MAKING UP

Work in all ends. Sew side and sleeve seams. Work a neat strengthening st to inside of neck edge where collar divides.

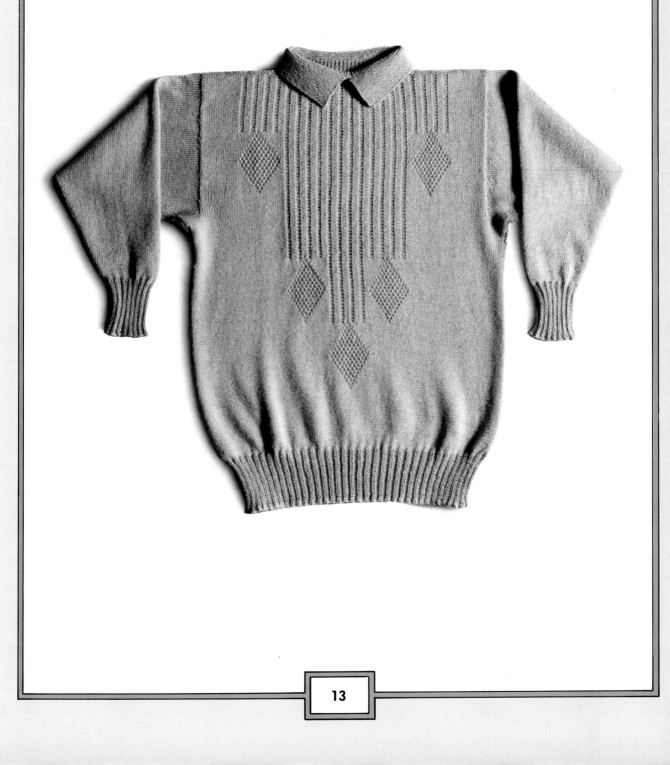

MAUD
Ladies waistcoat in 4 ply wool

A thoroughly modern waistcoat with just a thread of influence from the world of F. Scott Fitzgerald; lean and sophisticated with diamonds as big as The Ritz. The body is worked in stocking stitch patterned with moss stitch diamonds and garter stitch ladders with twisted rib used for the borders and welts. Deep armholes accommodate shirt sleeves comfortably.

MATERIALS
7 (8: 8: 9) 50 gm balls 4 ply wool
2 2¾ mm (12) needles
2 3¼ mm (10) needles
4 2¾ mm (12) double pointed needles
stitch holders
10 buttons 1 cm (½ in) diameter

MEASUREMENTS
Bust
86 (91: 97: 102) cm
34 (36: 38: 40) in
Actual measurement
99 (104: 109: 114) cm
39 (41: 43: 45) in
Finished length to shoulder
71 (71: 71: 71) cm
28 (28: 28: 28) in

TENSION
28 sts and 36 rows for a 10 cm (4 in) square worked in st.st on 3¼ mm (10) needles

BACK
With 2¾ mm (12) needles cast on 135 (143: 151: 159) sts. Work 9 cm (3½ in) in k1, p1 twisted rib (k into back of k sts). Change to 3¼ mm (10) needles and continue in st.st. Work 34 rows. Now work 1st part of pattern as follows:
1st row: with right side facing k 67 (71: 75: 79) sts, p1, k to end of row.
2nd row: p 67 (71: 75: 79) sts, k1, p to end of row.
3rd row: k 66 (70: 74: 78) sts, p1, k1, p1, k to end of row.

4th row: p 66 (70: 74: 78) sts, k1, p1, k1, p to end of row.
5th row: k 65 (69: 73: 77) sts, (p1, k1) 3 times, k to end of row.
6th row: p 65 (69: 73: 77) sts, (k1, p1) 3 times, p to end of row.
These last 6 rows set pattern. Continue as set inc the diamond by 2 sts every k row. Work 20 rows in all. Now work diamond in reverse as follows:
21st row: k 59 (63: 67: 71) sts, (p1, k1) 9 times, k to end of row.
22nd row: p 59 (63: 67: 71) sts, (k1, p1) 9 times, p to end of row.
23rd row: k 60 (64: 68: 72) sts, (p1, k1) 8 times, k to end of row.
24th row: p 60 (64: 68: 72) sts, (k1, p1) 8 times, p to end of row.
These last 4 rows set the pattern. Continue as set dec the diamond by 2 sts every k row until the 38th row has been worked. These 38 rows make the 1st part of the pattern. Now work the 2nd part as follows:
1st row: with right side facing k 47 (51: 55: 59) sts, p1, k11, (p2, k3) 3 times, p2, k11, p1, k to end of row.
2nd row: p 47 (51: 55: 59) sts, k1, p39, k1, p to end of row.
3rd row: k 46 (50: 54: 58) sts, p1, k1, p1, k10, (p2, k3) 3 times, p2, k10, p1, k1, p1, k to end of row.
4th row: p 46 (50: 54: 58) sts, k1, p1, k1, p37, k1, p1, k1, p to end of row.
5th row: k 45 (49: 53: 57) sts, (p1, k1) 3 times, k8, (p2, k3) 3 times, p2, k9, (p1, k1) 3 times, k to

end of row.
6th row: p 45 (49: 53: 57) sts, (k1, p1) 3 times, p34, (k1, p1) 3 times, p to end of row.
These last 6 rows set the pattern. Continue as set inc the 2 diamonds by 2 sts every k row. Work 20 rows in all. Now work pattern in reverse as follows:
21st row: k 39 (43: 47: 51) sts, (p1, k1) 9 times, k2, (p2, k3) 3 times, p2, k3, (p1, k1) 9 times, k to end of row.
22nd row: p39 (43: 47: 51) sts, (k1, p1) 9 times, p22, (k1, p1) 9 times, p to end of row.
23rd row: k 40 (44: 48: 52) sts, (p1, k1) 8 times, k3, (p2, k3) 3 times, p2, k4, (p1, k1) 8 times, k to end of row.
24th row: p 40 (44: 48: 52) sts, (k1, p1) 8 times, p24, (k1, p1) 8 times, p to end of row.
These last 4 rows set the pattern. Continue as set dec the 2 diamonds by 2 sts every k row until the 38th row has been worked. These 38 rows make the 2nd part of the pattern. Now work the 3rd part as follows:
1st row: with right side facing k 39 (43: 47: 51) sts, (p2, k3) 11 times, p2, k to end of row.
2nd row: p.
Repeat these last 2 rows 10 more times.
Shape armholes
With right side facing and working in pattern k the first 16 sts and put these sts on a s.st.h, work to last 16 sts and put them on a s.st.h. Turn and continue on remaining 103 (111: 119: 127) sts.
Next row: p.
Now work 14 more rows in pattern. These last 38 rows make the 3rd part of the pattern. Now work 4th part of pattern as follows:
1st row: with right side facing k 11 (15: 19: 23) sts, p1, k11, (p2, k3) 11 times, p2, k11, p1, k to end of row.
2nd row: p 11 (15: 19: 23) sts, k1, p79, k1, p to end of row.
3rd row: k 10 (14: 18: 22) sts, p1, k1, p1, k10, (p2, k3) 11 times, p2, k10, p1, k1, p1, k to end of row.
4th row: p 10 (14: 18: 22) sts, k1, p1, k1, p77, k1, p1, k1, p to end of row.
5th row: k 9 (13: 17: 21) sts, (p1, k1) 3 times, k8, (p2, k3) 11 times, p2, k9, (p1, k1) 3 times, k to end of row.
6th row: p 9 (13: 17: 21) sts, (k1, p1) 3 times, p74, (k1, p1) 3 times, p to end of row.
These last 6 rows set the pattern. Continue as

set inc the 2 diamonds by 2 sts every k row. Work 20 rows in all. Now work the diamonds in reverse as follows:
21st row: k 3 (7: 11: 15) sts, (p1, k1) 9 times, k2, (p2, k3) 11 times, p2, k3, (p1, k1) 9 times, k to end of row.
22nd row: p 3 (7: 11: 15) sts, (k1, p1) 9 times, p62, (k1, p1) 9 times, p to end of row.
23rd row: k 4 (8: 12: 16) sts, (p1, k1) 8 times, k3, (p2, k3) 11 times, p2, k4, (p1, k1) 8 times, k to end of row.
24th row: p 4 (8: 12: 16) sts, (k1, p1) 8 times, p64, (k1, p1) 8 times, p to end of row.
These last 4 rows set the pattern. Continue as set dec the 2 diamonds by 2 sts every k row until the 38th row has been worked. These 38 rows make the 4th part of the pattern. Now work the 5th part as follows:
1st row: with right side facing k 3 (7: 11: 15) sts, (p2, k3) 20 times, k to end of row.
2nd row: p.
Repeat these last 2 rows 14 more times.
Shape neck
With right side facing and keeping continuity of pattern correct
next row: work 43 (47: 51: 55) sts, turn and continue on these sts dec 1 st at neck edge on this and every row until 30 (34: 38: 42) sts remain. Leave sts on a s.st.h for shoulder seam, leave centre 17 sts on a s.st.h for back neck edge and continue on remaining 43 (47: 51: 55) sts, work to end of row. Now work to correspond with other side of neck reversing shaping.
Pocket linings
Work 2 the same. With 3¼ mm (10) needles cast on 35 sts. Work 50 rows in st.st and leave sts on a s.st.h.

LEFT FRONT
With 2¾ mm (12) needles cast on 73 (77: 81: 85) sts. Work in k1, p1 twisted rib working a k st at all edges and starting 1st row thus:
1st row: k2, *p1, k1; repeat from * to last st, k1.
Continue until rib measures 9 cm (3½ in).
Change to 3¼ mm (10) needles and continue in st.st.
next row: k to last 9 sts, put these on a st.st.h (for front border), turn and continue on remaining 64 (68: 72: 76) sts. Work until 50 rows have been worked in st.st.

Place pocket lining

With right side facing k7, slip next 35 sts on to a s.st.h and in place of these k across 35 sts of pocket lining, k to end of row. Continue straight until front corresponds to back length to start of 2nd part of pattern. Now work 2nd part of pattern on front thus:

1st row: with right side facing k 47 (51: 55: 59) sts, p1, k to end of row.

2nd row: p16, k1, p to end of row.

3rd row: k 46 (50: 54: 58) sts, p1, k1, p1, k to end of row.

4th row: p15, k1, p1, k1, p to end of row.

5th row: k 45 (49: 53: 57) sts, (p1, k1) 3 times, k to end of row.

6th row: p14, (k1, p1) 3 times, p to end of row. These last 6 rows set the pattern. Continue as set inc the diamond by 2 sts every k row. Work 20 rows in all. Now work diamond in reverse as follows:

21st row: k 39 (43: 47: 51) sts, (p1, k1) 9 times, k to end of row.

22nd row: p8, (k1, p1) 9 times, p to end of row.

23rd row: k 40 (44: 48: 52) sts, (p1, k1) 8 times, k to end of row.

24th row: p9, (k1, p1) 8 times, p to end of row. These last 4 rows set the pattern. Continue as set dec the diamond by 2 sts every k row until the 38th row has been worked. These 38 rows make the 2nd part of pattern for the front. Now work the 3rd part as follows:

1st row: with right side facing k 39 (43: 47: 51) sts, (p2, k3) 4 times, k to end of row.

2nd row: p.

Repeat these last 2 rows 10 more times.

Shape armhole

With right side facing k the first 16 sts and leave on a s.st.h. Work in pattern to end of row. (48: 52: 56: 60) sts. Continue in pattern on these sts until 38 rows of 3rd pattern are complete. Now work the 4th part of pattern as follows:

1st row: with right side facing k 11 (15: 19: 23) sts, p1, k11, (p2, k3) 4 times, k to end of row.

2nd row: p 36, k1, p to end of row.

3rd row: k 10 (14: 18: 22) sts, p1, k1, p1, k10, (p2, k3) 4 times, k to end of row.

4th row: p35, k1, p1, k1, p to end of row.

5th row: k 9 (13: 17: 21) sts, (p1, k1) 3 times, k8, (p2, k3) 4 times, k to end of row.

6th row: p34, (k1, p1) 3 times, p to end of row. These last 6 rows set the pattern. Continue as

set inc the diamond by 2 sts every k row. Work 20 rows in all. Now work in reverse as follows:

21st row: k 3 (7: 11: 15) sts, (p1, k1) 9 times, k2, (p2, k3) 4 times, k to end of row.

22nd row: p28, (k1, p1) 9 times, p to end of row.

23rd row: k 4 (8: 12: 16) sts, (p1, k1) 8 times, k3, (p2, k3) 4 times, k to end of row.

24th row: p29, (k1, p1) 8 times, p to end of row. These last 4 rows set the pattern. Continue as set dec the diamond by 2 sts every k row until the 38th row has been worked. These last 38 rows make the 4th part of the pattern. Now work the 5th part as follows *at the same time*

Shape front neck

1st row: with right side facing k 3 (7: 11: 15) sts, (p2, k3) 7 times, p2, k1, turn, leaving remaining 7 sts on a s.st.h for front neck edge. Continue on remaining 41 (45: 49: 53) sts.

2nd row: p.

These 2 rows set the position of the pattern for the 5th part. Keeping continuity of pattern correct dec 1 st at neck edge on the next and every following row until 30 (34: 38: 42) sts remain. Now work straight in pattern until front length corresponds to back. Leave sts on a s.st.h for shoulder seam.

To make a buttonhole

With right side facing k2, p1, k1, yfwd, k2 tog, work to end of row.

RIGHT FRONT

Work the same as left reversing pattern all shapings and *pocket position* and working 2 buttonholes into the ribbing, the first 1 cm (½ in), the second 8 cm (3 in) from cast on edge.

Shoulder seam

Work 2 the same. With 3¼ mm (10) needles put 30 (34: 38: 42) sts from the back and the same from the front on to spare needles. Place these 2 needles side by side with the wrong sides of work facing each other. Then working on the right side of work, k tog a st from each needle to give 1 st on right hand needle. *K tog the next 2 sts (now 2 sts on right hand needle) then pass the 1st of these 2 sts over the 2nd. Repeat from * to work rest of the sts.

FRONT BORDERS

Left side

With 2¾ mm (12) needles pick up the 9 sts on s.st.h and work in k1, p1 twisted rib working a k st at all edges. Continue until border measures 5 cm (2 in) less than front edge. Leave the 9 sts on a s.st.h. Mark the button positions, the first 1 cm (½ in), the second 8 cm (3 in) from cast on edge and 7 more evenly spaced allowing for a 10th buttonhole in neck edge.

Right side

Work the same as left, working buttonholes to correspond to button positions.

Neck edge

With right side facing and 2¾ mm (12) needles, start at right front border and rib 9 sts from s.st.h, k across 7 sts on s.st.h (front neck edge), pick up and k 41 sts up side front, 1 st from shoulder seam, 12 sts down side back, 17 sts from s.st.h (back neck edge), 12 sts up side back, 1 st from shoulder seam, 41 sts down side front, 7 sts on s.st.h and rib across 9 sts of left front border. (157 sts). Work 9 rows in k1, p1 twisted rib working a buttonhole on the 4th row. Cast off loosely in rib.

Pocket tops

Work 2 the same. With 2¾ mm (12) needles pick up and k the 35 sts on s.st.h. Work 9 rows in k1, p1 twisted rib. Cast off loosely in rib.

ARMHOLE EDGES

Work 2 the same. With right side of work facing and 4 2¾ mm (12) double pointed needles, pick up and k 16 sts from s.st.h (armhole shaping), 158 sts evenly along armhole edge with centre st at shoulder seam and 16 sts from s.st.h. (190 sts). Work 9 rounds in k1, p1 rib (every other row twisted). Cast off loosely in rib.

MAKING UP

Work in all ends. Sew borders to fronts working the ease in equally, sew side seams, pocket top edges to fronts, pocket linings to inside of fronts and buttons to positions as marked.

AGATHA
Ladies cardigan in 4 ply wool

The last of the trio of diamonds, proving that a girl's best friend is sometimes her cardigan. Its scooped, round neck make it a perfect partner for Emily, and the ladder and diamond pattern echo hers exactly. Twisted rib gives a crisp finish to the welts, cuffs and pocket tops.

MATERIALS
11 (11: 12: 12) 50 gm balls 4 ply wool
2 2¾ mm (12) needles
2 3¼ mm (10) needles
stitch holders
10 buttons 1 cm (½ in) diameter

MEASUREMENTS
Bust
86 (91: 97: 102) cm
34 (36: 38: 40) in
Actual measurement
98 (104: 109: 114) cm
38½ (41: 43: 45) in
Finished length to shoulder
71 (71: 71: 71) cm
28 (28: 28: 28) in
Sleeve length
52 (53: 54: 54) cm
20½ (21: 21½: 21½) in

TENSION
28 sts and 36 rows for a 10 cm (4 in) square worked in st.st on 3¼ mm (10) needles

BACK
With 2¾ mm (12) needles cast on 135 (143: 151: 159) sts. Work 9 cm (3½ in) in k1, p1 twisted rib (k into back of k st). Change to 3¼ mm (10) and continue in st.st. Work 34 rows. Now work 1st part of pattern as follows:
1st row: k 67 (71: 75: 79) sts, p1, k to end of row.
2nd row: p 67 (71: 75: 79) sts, k1, p to end of row.
3rd row: k 66 (70: 74: 78) sts, p1, k1, p1, k to end of row.

4th row: p 66 (70: 74: 78) sts, k1, p1, k1, p to end of row.
5th row: k 65 (69: 73: 77) sts, (p1, k1) 3 times, k to end of row.
6th row: p 65 (69: 73: 77) sts, (k1, p1) 3 times, p to end of row.
These last 6 rows set pattern. Continue as set inc the diamond by 2 sts every k row. Work 20 rows in all. Now work diamond in reverse as follows:
21st row: k 59 (63: 67: 71) sts, (p1, k1) 9 times, k to end of row.
22nd row: p 59 (63: 67: 71) sts, (k1, p1) 9 times, p to end of row.
23rd row: k 60 (64: 68: 72) sts, (p1, k1) 8 times, k to end of row.
24th row: p 60 (64: 68: 72) sts, (k1, p1) 8 times, p to end of row.
These last 4 rows set the pattern. Continue as set dec the diamond by 2 sts every k row until the 38th row has been worked. These 38 rows make the first part of the pattern. Now work the 2nd part as follows:
1st row: with right side facing k 47 (51: 55: 59) sts, p1, k11, (p2, k3) 3 times, p2, k11, p1, k to end of row.
2nd row: p 47 (51: 55: 59) sts, k1, p39, k1, p to end of row.
3rd row: k 46 (50: 54: 58) sts, p1, k1, p1, k10, (p2, k3) 3 times, p2, k10, p1, k1, p1, k to end of row.
4th row: p 46 (50: 54: 58) sts, k1, p1, k1, p37, k1, p1, k1, p to end of row.
5th row: k 45 (49: 53: 57) sts, (p1, k1) 3 times, k8, (p2, k3) 3 times, p2, k9, (p1, k1) 3 times, k to end of row.
6th row: p 45 (49: 53: 57) sts, (k1, p1) 3 times,

p34, (k1, p1) 3 times, p to end of row.
These last 6 rows set the pattern. Continue as set inc the 2 diamonds by 2 sts every k row. Work 20 rows in all. Now work pattern in reverse as follows:

21st row: k 39 (43: 47: 51) sts, (p1, k1) 9 times, k2, (p2, k3) 3 times, p2, k3, (p1, k1) 9 times, k to end of row.

22nd row: p 39 (43: 47: 51) sts, (k1, p1) 9 times, p22, (k1, p1) 9 times, p to end of row.

23rd row: k 40 (44: 48: 52) sts, (p1, k1) 8 times, k3, (p2, k3) 3 times, p2, k4, (p1, k1) 8 times, k to end of row.

24th row: p 40 (44: 48: 52) sts, (k1, p1) 8 times, p24, (k1, p1) 8 times, p to end of row.
These last 4 rows set the pattern. Continue as set dec the 2 diamonds by 2 sts every k row until the 38th row has been worked. These 38 rows make the 2nd part of the pattern. Now work the 3rd part as follows:

1st row: with right side facing k 39 (43: 47: 51) sts, (p2, k3) 11 times, p2, k to end of row.

2nd row: p.
Repeat these last 2 rows 11 more times.

Shape armholes
With right side facing and working in pattern k the first 9 sts and put these sts on a s.st.h, work to last 9 sts and put them on a s.st.h. Turn and continue on remaining 117 (125: 133: 141) sts. Now work 13 more rows in pattern. These last 38 rows make the 3rd part of the pattern. Now work 4th part of pattern as follows:

1st row: with right side facing k 18 (22: 26: 30) sts, p1, k11, (p2, k3) 11 times, p2, k11, p1, k to end of row.

2nd row: p 18 (22: 26: 30) sts, k1, p79, k1, p to end of row.

3rd row: k 17 (21: 25: 29) sts, p1, k1, p1, k10, (p2, k3) 11 times, p2, k10, p1, k1, p1, k to end of row.

4th row: p 17 (21: 25: 29) sts, k1, p1, k1, p77, k1, p1, k1, p to end of row.

5th row: k 16 (20: 24: 28) sts, (p1, k1) 3 times, k8, (p2, k3) 11 times, p2, k9, (p1, k1) 3 times, k to end of row.

6th row: p 16 (20: 24: 28) sts, (k1, p1) 3 times, p74, (k1, p1) 3 times, p to end of row.
These last 6 rows set the pattern. Continue as set inc the 2 diamonds by 2 sts every k row. Work 20 rows in all. Now work the diamonds in reverse as follows:

21st row: k 10 (14: 18: 22) sts, (p1, k1) 9 times, k2, (p2, k3) 11 times, p2, k3, (p1, k1) 9 times, k to end of row.

22nd row: p 10 (14: 18: 22) sts, (k1, p1) 9 times, p62, (k1, p1) 9 times, p to end of row.

23rd row: k 11 (15: 19: 23) sts, (p1, k1) 8 times, k3, (p2, k3) 11 times, p2, k4, (p1, k1) 8 times, k to end of row.

24th row: p 11 (15: 19: 23) sts, (k1, p1) 8 times, p 64, (k1, p1) 8 times, p to end of row.
These last 4 rows set the pattern. Continue as set dec the 2 diamonds by 2 sts every k row until the 38th row has been worked. These 38 rows make the 4th part of the pattern. Now work the 5th part as follows:

1st row: with right side facing k 10 (14: 18: 22) sts, (p2, k3) 20 times, k to end of row.

2nd row: p.
Repeat these last 2 rows 14 more times.

Shape neck
With right side facing and keeping continuity of pattern correct

next row: work 50 (54: 58: 62) sts, turn and continue on these sts dec 1 st at neck edge on this and every row until 37 (41: 45: 49) sts remain. Leave sts on a s.st.h for shoulder seam, leave centre 17 sts on a s.st.h for back neck edge and continue on remaining 50 (54: 58: 62) sts, work to end of row. Now work to correspond with other side of neck reversing shaping.

Pocket linings
Work 2 the same. With 3¼ mm (10) needles cast on 35 sts. Work 44 rows in st.st and leave sts on a s.st.h.

LEFT FRONT

With 2¾ mm (12) needles cast on 73 (77: 81: 85) sts. Work in k1, p1 twisted rib working a k st at all edges and starting first row thus:

1st row: k2, *p1, k1; repeat from * to last st, k1.
Continue until rib measures 9 cm (3½ in).
Change to 3¼ mm (10) needles and continue in st.st.

1st row: k to last 9 sts, put these on a st.st.h (for front border), turn and continue on remaining 64 (68: 72: 76) sts. Work until 44 rows have been worked in st.st.

Place pocket lining
With right side facing k7, slip next 35 sts on to a s.st.h and in place of these k across 35 sts of

pocket lining, k to end of row. Continue straight until front corresponds to back length at start of second part of pattern. Now work 2nd part of pattern on front thus:

1st row: with right side facing k 47 (51: 55: 59) sts, p1, k to end of row.
2nd row: p16, k1, p to end of row.
3rd row: k 46 (50: 54: 58) sts, p1, k1, p1, k to end of row.
4th row: p15, k1, p1, k1, p to end of row.
5th row: k 45 (49: 53: 57) sts, (p1, k1) 3 times, k to end of row.
6th row: p14, (k1, p1) 3 times, p to end of row.
These last 6 rows set the pattern. Continue as set inc the diamond by 2 sts every k row. Work 20 rows in all. Now work diamond in reverse as follows:

21st row: k 39 (43: 47: 51) sts, (p1, k1) 9 times, k to end of row.
22nd row: p8, (k1, p1) 9 times, p to end of row.
23rd row: k 40 (44: 48: 52) sts, (p1, k1) 8 times, k to end of row.
24th row: p9, (k1, p1) 8 times, p to end of row.
These last 4 rows set the pattern. Continue as set dec the diamond by 2 sts every k row until the 38th row has been worked. These 38 rows make the 2nd part of pattern for the front. Now work the 3rd part as follows:

1st row: with right side facing k 39 (43: 47: 51) sts, (p2, k3) 4 times, k to end of row.
2nd row: p.
Repeat these last 2 rows 11 more times.

Shape armhole
With right side facing k the first 9 sts and leave on a s.st.h. Work in pattern to end of row. (55: 59: 63: 67) sts. Continue in pattern on these sts for 13 more rows. These last 38 rows make the 3rd part of pattern. Now work the 4th part of pattern as follows:

1st row: with right side facing k 18 (22: 26: 30) sts, p1, k11, (p2, k3) 4 times, k to end of row.
2nd row: p 36, k1, p to end of row.
3rd row: k 17 (21: 25: 29) sts, p1, k1, p1, k10, (p2, k3) 4 times, k to end of row.
4th row: p35, k1, p1, k1, p to end of row.
5th row: k 16 (20: 24: 28) sts, (p1, k1) 3 times, k8, (p2, k3) 4 times, k to end of row.
6th row: p34, (k1, p1) 3 times, p to end of row.
These last 6 rows set the pattern. Continue as set inc the diamond by 2 sts every k row. Work 20 rows in all. Now work in reverse as follows:

21st row: k 10 (14: 18: 22) sts, (p1, k1) 9 times, k2, (p2, k3) 4 times, k to end of row.
22nd row: p28, (k1, p1) 9 times, p to end of row.
23rd row: k 11 (15: 19: 23) sts, (p1, k1) 8 times, k3, (p2, k3) 4 times, k to end of row.
24th row: p29, (k1, p1) 8 times, p to end of row.
These last 4 rows set the pattern. Continue as set dec the diamond by 2 sts every k row until the 38th row has been worked. These last 38 rows make the 4th part of the pattern. Now work the 5th part as follows *at the same time*.

Shape front neck
1st row: with right side facing k 10 (14: 18: 22) sts, (p2, k3) 7 times, p2, k1, turn, leaving remaining 7 sts on a s.st.h for front neck edge. Continue on remaining 48 (52: 56: 60) sts.
2nd row: p.
These 2 rows set the position of the pattern for the 5th part. Keeping continuity of pattern correct dec 1 st at neck edge on the next and every following row until 37 (41: 45: 49) sts remain. Now work straight in pattern until front length corresponds to back. Leave sts on a s.st.h for shoulder seam.

To make a buttonhole
With right side facing k2, p1, k1, yfwd, k2 tog, work to end of row.

RIGHT FRONT
Work the same as left reversing pattern, all shapings and *pocket position* and working 2 buttonholes into the ribbing, the 1st 1 cm (½ in), the 2nd 8 cm (3 in) from cast on edge.

Shoulder seam
Work 2 the same. With 3¼ mm (10) needles put 37 (41: 45: 49) sts from the back and the same from the front on to spare needles. Place these 2 needles side by side with the wrong sides of work facing each other. Then working on the right side of work, k tog a st from each needle to give 1 st on right hand needle. *K tog the next 2 sts (now 2 sts on right hand needle) then pass the 1st of these 2 sts over the 2nd. Repeat from * to work rest of the sts.

FRONT BORDERS
Left side
With 2¾ mm (12) needles pick up the 9 sts on

s.st.h and work in k1, p1 twisted rib working a k st at all edges. Continue until border measures 5 cm (2 in) less than front edge. Leave the 9 sts on a s.st.h. Mark the button positions, the 1st 1 cm (½ in), the 2nd 8 cm (3 in) from cast on edge and 7 more evenly spaced allowing for a 10th buttonhole in neck edge.

Right side
Work the same as left, working buttonholes to correspond to button positions.

Neck edge
With right side facing and 2¾ mm (12) needles start at right front border, rib 9 sts from s.st.h, k across 7 sts on s.st.h (front neck edge), pick up and k 41 sts up side front, 1 st from shoulder seam, 12 sts down side back, 17 sts from s.st.h (back neck edge), 12 sts up side back, 1 st from shoulder seam, 41 sts down side front, 7 sts on s.st.h and rib across 9 sts of left front border. (157 sts). Work 9 rows in k1, p1 twisted rib working a buttonhole on the 4th row. Cast off loosely in rib.

Pocket tops
Work 2 the same. With 2¾ mm (12) needles pick up and k the 35 sts on s.st.h. Work 9 rows in k1, p1 twisted rib. Cast off loosely in rib.

SLEEVES
Work 2 the same. With right side facing and 3¼ mm (10) needles, pick up and k 9 sts from s.st.h (armhole shaping), 139 sts evenly along armhole edge with centre st at shoulder seam and 9 sts from s.st.h. (157 sts). Then dec 1 st at each end of every 4th row as follows:
k2, sl.1, k1, psso, k to last 4 sts, k2 tog, k2 until 79 (77: 75: 75) sts remain.

Shape cuff
With wrong side facing dec 27 (21: 15: 11) sts evenly across row. (52: 56: 60: 64) sts. Change to 2¾ mm (12) needles and work 9 cm (3½ in) in k1, p1 twisted rib. Cast off loosely in rib.

MAKING UP
Work in all ends. Sew borders to fronts working the ease in equally, sew side and sleeve seams, pocket top edges to fronts, pocket linings to inside of fronts and buttons to positions as marked.

SCHOOLDAYS
Ladies sweater in 4 ply wool

A long, tunic line sweater, very flattering and easy to wear, knitted in mock moss stitch. The neckline is worked in three different stitches: reverse stocking stitch ribs running from shoulder to shoulder, rib for the collar stand and garter stitch for the collar. The armholes are edged in reverse stocking stitch rib for added definition.

MATERIALS
10 (11: 11: 12) 50 gm balls 4 ply wool
2 2¾ mm (12) needles
2 3 mm (11) needles
2 3¼ mm (10) needles
4 2¾ mm (12) double pointed needles
stitch holders

MEASUREMENTS
Bust
86 (91: 97: 102) cm
34 (36: 38: 40) in
Measurement at widest point
90 (97: 103: 109) cm
35½ (38: 40½: 43) in
Length to shoulder
71 (72: 73: 74) cm
28 (28½: 29: 29½) in
Sleeve length
52 (53: 54: 54) cm
20½ (21: 21½: 21½) in

TENSION
26 sts and 44 rows for a 10 cm (4 in) square worked in pattern on 3¼ mm (10) needles

BACK AND FRONT
Both the same. With 2¾ mm (12) needles cast on 116 (124: 132: 140) sts. Work 30 rows in g.st. Change to 3¼ mm (10) needles and continue in pattern as follows:
1st row: with right side facing *p2, k2; repeat from * to end of row.
2nd row: p.
3rd row: *k2, p2; repeat from * to end of row.
4th row: p.

These 4 rows make 1 pattern. Continue keeping continuity of pattern correct until work measures 46 cm (18 in) from cast on edge.
Shape armholes
With right side facing and keeping continuity of pattern correct
next row: work the 1st 8 sts and put them on a s.st.h, work to last 8 sts and put these on a s.st.h. Turn and continue on remaining 100 (108: 116: 124) sts. Work straight for 91 (97: 103: 109) rows. Change to 3 mm (11) needles. With right side facing work 3 rows in r.st.st then 2 rows in st.st. Repeat these 5 rows 3 times more. Leave all sts on a s.st.h for shoulder seams and collar.

Close-up of stitch detail (actual size)

Shoulder seam

Work 2 the same. With 3¼ mm (10) needles put 22 (25: 28: 31) sts from the back and the same from the front on to spare needles. Place these 2 needles side by side with wrong sides of work facing each other. Then working on the right side of work, k tog a st from each needle to give 1 st on right hand needle. *K tog the next 2 sts (now 2 sts on right hand needle) then pass the 1st of these 2 sts over the 2nd. Repeat from * to work the rest of the sts.

COLLAR

With right side facing and 4 2¾ mm (12) double pointed needles, put the sts for the neck plus 2 sts (1 from each shoulder seam) on 3 of the needles allowing for collar opening at centre front. (114: 118: 122: 126) sts. Start at centre front and work 10 rounds in k1, p1 rib. Now divide for collar and work in rows. At centre front, turn and continue in g.st until collar measures 9 cm (3½ in) from pick up row. With wrong side of collar facing, cast off so that the collar edge neither frills nor is too tight.

SLEEVES

Work 2 the same. With right side facing and 3 mm (11) needles, pick up and k 8 sts from s.st.h, 55 (59: 63: 67) sts evenly along armhole edge to shoulder ribs, 21 sts over shoulder ribs with centre st at shoulder seam, 54 (58: 62: 66) sts to armhole shaping and 8 sts from s.st.h. (146: 154: 162: 170) sts.

next row: p.

Work next 3 rows in r.st.st. Work 1 row p. Change to 3¼ mm (10) needles and continue in pattern as given for front and back, dec 1 st at each end of the next and every 5th row. Start first row of pattern thus:

k1, *p2, k2; repeat from * to last st, p1.

This sets the position of the pattern. Continue until 72 (78: 82: 90) sts remain and work measures 43 (44: 45: 45) cm 17 (17½: 18: 18) in.

Shape cuff

With wrong side facing

next row: dec 20 (24: 26: 30) sts evenly across row. (52: 54: 56: 60) sts.

Change to 2¾ mm (12) needles and work 9 cm (3½ in) in k2, p2 rib. Cast off loosely in rib.

MAKING UP

Work in all ends, sew sleeve and side seams. Work a neat strengthening stitch on inside of neck edge where collar divides.

GAMES

Sweater for men and women in 4 ply wool

This is the sweater to make the best days of your life go on and on and on . . . Based on the classic schoolboy's sports jersey, it is loose, easy and timeless. Worked in stocking stitch, the body is fully fashioned to the waist and the fully fashioned shirt collar is ribbed on to the straight-across neck.

MATERIALS

Ladies
10 (10: 11: 11) 50 gm balls 4 ply wool
Men
10 (11: 11: 12: 12) 50 gm balls 4 ply wool
2 2¾ mm (12) needles
2 3¼ mm (10) needles
4 2¾ mm (12) double pointed needles
4 3¼ mm (10) double pointed needles
stitch holders

MEASUREMENTS

Bust
86 (91: 97: 102) cm
34 (36: 38: 40) in
Actual measurement
103 (109: 114: 119) cm
40½ (43: 45: 47) in
Finished length to shoulder
65 (66: 67: 68) cm
25½ (26: 26½: 27) in
Sleeve length
47 (48: 49: 49) cm
18½ (19: 19½: 19½) in
Chest
91 (97: 102: 107: 112) cm
36 (38: 40: 42: 44) in
Actual measurement
109 (114: 119: 125: 132) cm
43 (45: 47: 49½: 52) in
Finished length to shoulder
66 (67: 68: 69: 70) cm
26 (26½: 27: 27½: 28) in
Sleeve length
54 (55: 56: 56: 56) cm
21 (21½: 22: 22: 22) in

TENSION

28 sts and 36 rows for a 10 cm (4 in) square worked in st.st on 3¼ mm (10) needles

BACK AND FRONT

Both the same. With 2¾ mm (12) needles cast on 114 (122: 130: 138: 146: 154) sts. Work 9 cm (3½ in) in k2, p2 rib. Change to 3¼ mm (10) needles and continue in st.st inc 1 st at each end of 3rd and then every 4th row as follows: with right side facing k2, inc into next st, k to the last 4 sts, inc into next st, k3
until 142 (150: 158: 166: 174: 182) sts are on the needle. Continue working straight on these sts until work measures 43 cm (17 in) from cast on edge.

Shape armholes
With right side facing knit the first 9 sts and put on a s.st.h, k to last 9 sts and put these on a s.st.h. (124: 132: 140: 148: 156: 164) sts. Turn and continue straight on these sts for 77 (81: 85: 89: 93: 97) rows.
Leave these sts on a s.st.h for the shoulder seams and collar.

Shoulder seam
Work 2 the same. With 3¼ mm (10) needles put 32 (35: 38: 41: 44: 47) sts from the back and the same number from the front on to spare needles. Place these 2 needles side by side with the wrong sides of work facing each other. Then working on the right side of work, k tog a st from each needle to give 1 st on right hand needle. *K tog the next 2 sts (now 2 sts on right hand needle) then pass the 1st of these 2 sts over the 2nd. Repeat from * to work the rest of the sts.

COLLAR

With right side facing and 4 2¾ mm (12) double pointed needles, pick up and k 60 (62: 64: 66: 68: 70) sts from s.st.h (front neck edge), 1 st from shoulder seam, 60 (62: 64: 66: 68: 70) sts from s.st.h (back neck edge) and 1 st from shoulder seam. (122: 126: 130: 134: 138: 142) sts. Work 11 rounds in k1, p1 rib keeping the 2

4th row: as 2nd row.

Continue repeating these 4 rows until collar measures 9 cm (3½ in) from pick up row. Work 2 more rows without increasing. Cast off loosely in rib.

SLEEVES

Work 2 the same. With right side facing and

centre front sts as k sts and making 1 extra st at centre back on first row only. Now divide for collar. Change to 4 size 3¼ mm (10) double pointed needles, turn work and work in rows thus:

1st row: k1, *k1, p1; repeat from * to last 2 sts, k2.

2nd row: (k1, p1) twice, inc into next st, rib to last 6 sts, inc into next st, rib to end of row.

3rd row: k2, p1, k1, p2, rib to last 6 sts, p2, k1, p1, k2.

3¼ mm (10) needles, pick up and k 9 sts from s.st.h (armhole shaping), 113 (121: 129: 137: 145: 153) sts along armhole edge with centre st at shoulder seam and 9 sts from s.st.h. (131: 139: 147: 155: 163: 171) sts. Continuing in st.st dec 1 st at each end of 4th and every following (**Ladies**) 4th row (all sizes) until 63 (69: 75: 83) sts remain and work measures 38 (39: 40: 40) cm, 15 (15½: 16: 16) in.

(**Men**) 5th (5th: 5th: 4th: 4th) row thus:

on k rows: k2, sl.1, k1, psso, k to last 4 sts, k2 tog, k2.

on p rows: p2, p2 tog, p to last 4 sts, p2 tog tbl, p2.

until 77 (83: 89: 81: 89) sts remain and work measures 45 (46: 47: 47: 47) cm, 17½ (18: 18½: 18½: 18½) in.

Shape cuff

Dec evenly across the row (**ladies**) 9 (13: 17: 23) sts, (**men**) 15 (19: 23: 13: 19) sts to leave (**ladies**) 54 (56: 58: 60) sts, (**men**) 62 (64: 66: 68: 70) sts. Change to 2¾ mm (12) needles and work 9 cm (3½ in) in k2, p2 rib. Cast off loosely in rib.

MAKING UP

Work in all ends. Sew side and sleeve seams. Work a neat oversew strengthening stitch on the inside of centre front neck where the collar divides.

SWEAT SHIRT
Child's sweater in double knit wool, for 4 to 10 years

This is a simple, bloused, chunky shape based on every child's favourite, the sweat shirt. It looks great in strong, bright colours possibly with a contrasting colour used for the ribs and neckband or even knitted in bands of football colours. Just the thing for school.

MATERIALS
6 (7: 8: 9) 50 gm balls double knit wool
2 3¼ mm (10) needles
2 4 mm (8) needles
4 3¼ mm (10) double pointed needles
stitch holders

MEASUREMENTS
Chest
66 (71: 76: 81) cm
26 (28: 30: 32) in
Actual measurement
79 (84: 89: 94) cm
31 (33: 35: 37) in
Finished length to shoulder
43 (47: 51: 55) cm
17 (18½: 20: 21½) in
Sleeve length
37 (41: 44: 48) cm
14½ (16: 17½: 19) in

TENSION
22 sts and 30 rows for a 10 cm (4 in) square worked in st.st on 4 mm (8) needles

BACK
*With 3¼ mm (10) needles cast on 70 (76: 82: 88) sts. Work 6 cm (2½ in) in k2, p2 rib.
next row: inc 15 sts evenly across the row. (85: 91: 97: 103) sts. Change to 4 mm (8) needles and continue in st.st until work measures 29 (31: 33: 35) cm, 11 (12: 13: 14) in from cast on edge.
Shape armholes
With right side facing k 6 sts and put these sts on a s.st.h, k to last 6 sts and put these sts on a s.st.h, turn and continue on the remaining 73

(79: 85: 91) sts.* Work straight for 37 (41: 45: 49) rows.
Shape neck
With right side facing
next row: k 29 (31: 33: 35) sts, turn and continue on these sts dec 1 st every row as follows:
on p rows: p2, p2 tog, p to end of row.
on k rows: k to last 4 sts, k2 tog, k2.
Work until 22 (24: 26: 28) sts remain. Leave sts on s.st.h for shoulder seam. Leave centre 15 (17: 19: 21) sts on a s.st.h for neck edge. Rejoin yarn and continue on remaining 29 (31: 33: 35) sts. K to end of row. Work to match other side working dec rows as follows:
on p rows: p to last 4 sts, p2 tog tbl, p2.
on k rows: k2, sl.1, k1, psso, k to end of row.

FRONT
Work the same as Back from * to *. Work straight for 23 (27: 31: 35) rows.
Shape neck
With right side facing
next row: k 29 (31: 33: 35) sts, turn and continue on these sts dec 1 st at neck edge every row as follows:
on p rows: p2, p2 tog, p to end of row.
on k rows: k to last 4 sts, k2 tog, k2 until 22 (24: 26: 28) sts remain.
Work straight until front corresponds to back length (14 rows). Leave sts on a s.st.h for shoulder seam. Leave centre 15 (17: 19: 21) sts on a s.st.h for front neck edge. Rejoin wool to remaining 29 (31: 33: 35) sts and work to match other side working dec rows as follows:
on p rows: p to last 4 sts, p2 tog tbl, p2.
on k rows: k2, sl.1, k1, psso, k to end of row.

Shoulder seams

Work 2 the same. With 4 mm (8) needles put 22 (24: 26: 28) sts from the back and the same from the front on to spare needles. Place these 2 needles side by side with wrong sides of work facing each other. Then working on the right side of work, k tog a st from each needle to give 1 st on right hand needle. *K tog the next 2 sts (now 2 sts on right hand needle) then pass the 1st of these 2 sts over the 2nd. Repeat from * to work the rest of the sts.

Neck edge

With right side facing and 4 3¼ mm (10) double pointed needles, pick up and k 1 st at shoulder seam, 7 sts down side back, 15 (17: 19: 21) sts on s.st.h (back neck edge), 7 sts up side back, 1 st at shoulder seam, 20 sts down side front, 15 (17: 19: 21) sts on s.st.h (front neck edge) and 20 sts up side front. (86: 90: 94: 98) sts. Work 14 rounds in k1, p1 rib. Cast off loosely in rib. *Make sure that a child can get its head through*.

SLEEVES

Work 2 the same. With right side facing and 4 mm (8) needles pick up and k 6 sts on s.st.h (armhole shaping), 65 (71: 77: 83) sts evenly along armhole edge with centre stitch at shoulder seam, and 6 sts on s.st.h (armhole shaping). (77: 83: 89: 95) sts. Now dec 1 st at each end of every 5th row as follows:

on k rows: k2, sl.1, k1, psso, k to last 4 sts, k2 tog, k2.

on p rows: p2, p2 tog, p to last 4 sts, p2 tog tbl, p2.

until 41 (43: 45: 45) sts remain and work measures 31 (35: 38: 42) cm 12 (13½: 15: 16½) in.

Shape cuff

With wrong side facing dec 11 (11: 11: 9) sts evenly across row. (30: 32: 34: 36) sts. Change to 3¼ mm (10) needles and work 6 cm (2½ in) in k2, p2 rib. Cast off loosely in rib.

MAKING UP

Work in all ends, sew side and sleeve seams, sew cast off edge of neck rib to inside of work. Do make sure not to sew the rib edge tightly or it will not stretch sufficiently.

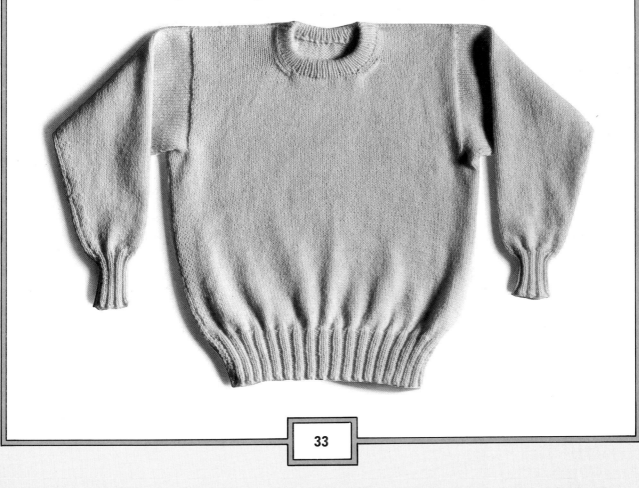

CLASSIC CARDIGAN
Ladies cardigan in 4 ply wool

The thoroughly British cardigan with all the hallmarks of tradition. It is fully fashioned and knitted in stocking stitch while the deep welts, cuffs, pocket tops and edges are in twisted rib. The neat pocket is just made for a lace handkerchief. Ideal to team with the Classic Jumper as the perfect classic twinset.

MATERIALS
10 (10: 11: 11) 50 gm balls 4 ply wool
2 2¾ mm (12) needles
2 3¼ mm (10) needles
stitch holders
10 buttons 1.5 cm (½ in) diameter

MEASUREMENTS
Bust
86 ((91: 97: 102) cm
34 (36: 38: 40) in
Actual measurement
99 (104: 109: 114) cm
39 (41: 43: 45) in
Finished length to shoulder
60 (61: 62: 63) cm
23½ (24: 24½: 25) in
Sleeve length
55 (56: 57: 57) cm
21½ (22: 22½: 22½) in

TENSION
28 sts and 36 rows for a 10 cm (4 in) square worked in st.st on 3¼ mm (10) needles

BACK
With 2¾ mm (12) needles cast on 117 (125: 133: 141) sts. Work 11 cm (4½ in) in k1, p1 twisted rib (k into back of k st). Change to 3¼ mm (10) needles and continue in st.st, inc 1 st at each end of the 9th and every following 10th row as follows:
k2, inc into next st, k to last 4 sts, inc into next st, k3
until there are 137 (145: 153: 161) sts.
Work 4 more rows or until work measures approx 41 cm (16 in) from cast on edge.
Shape armholes
With right side facing work 7 sts at the beginning of the next 2 rows and put them on s.st.h. (123: 131: 139: 147) sts remain. Continue straight for 62 (66: 70: 74) rows.
Shape neck
With right side facing k 39 (42: 45: 48) sts, turn and continue on these sts. Work 3 rows and leave sts on s.st.h for shoulder seam. Leave next 45 (47: 49: 51) sts on s.st.h for back neck edge. Rejoin yarn and work remaining 39 (42: 45: 48) sts to match other side.
Pocket lining for left front
With 3¼ mm (10) needles cast on 20 sts and work 7½ cm (3 in) in st.st. Leave sts on s.st.h.

LEFT FRONT
With 2¾ mm (12) needles cast on 65 (69: 73: 77) sts. Work in k1, p1 twisted rib (k into back of k sts) and work a k st at all edges starting 1st row thus:
k2, *p1, k1; repeat from * to last st, k1.
Continue until rib measures 11 cm (4½ in).
Change to 3¼ mm (10) needles and continue in st.st.
1st row: k to last 11 sts, put these on s.st.h for front border, turn and continue on remaining 54 (58: 62: 66) sts inc 1 st at side edge of 8th and every following 10th row as follows:
k2, inc into next st, k to end of row until there are 64 (68: 72: 76) sts. Work a further 4 rows. Front should now correspond to back length.
Shape armholes
With right side facing k 7 sts and put them on a s.st.h, k to end of row. (57: 61: 65: 69) sts

34

remain. Work 1 row.
Place pocket lining
With right side facing and working from armhole edge k 13 (17: 21: 25) sts, sl. next 20 sts on to a s.st.h and in place of these k across the 20 sts of the pocket lining. K to end of row. Continue straight for a further 29 (33: 37: 41) rows.

To make a buttonhole
With right side facing k2, (p1, k1) twice, yarn round needle, k2 tog, work to end of row.

RIGHT FRONT
Work as for left front *omitting the pocket* and reversing the shapings while working 3 buttonholes into the rib, the 1st being 1 cm (½

Shape neck
With right side facing work to the last 8 (9: 10: 11) sts and put these on a s.st.h (front neck edge), turn, and continue on remaining 49 (52: 55: 58) sts. Work to end of row.
1st row: p2, p2 tog, p to end of row.
2nd row: k to last 4 sts, k2 tog, k2.
Repeat these 2 rows until 39 (42: 45: 48) sts remain. Continue straight for 25 rows when work should correspond to back length. Leave sts on a s.st.h for shoulder seam.

in), the 2nd 6 cm (2½ in) from cast on edge and the 3rd on the last but one row of ribbing.
Work inc rows thus:
k to last 4 sts, inc into next st, k3.
Work neck dec thus:
1st row: p to last 4 sts, p2 tog tbl, p2.
2nd row: k2, sl.1, k1, psso, k to end of row.

FRONT BORDERS
Left side
With 2¾ mm (12) needles pick up the 11 sts on

s.st.h and work in k1, p1 twisted rib working a k st at all edges. Work until border measures 4 cm (1½ in) less than front edge. Leave the 11 sts on a s.st.h. Mark the button positions the 1st 1 cm (½ in), the 2nd 6 cm (2½ in), the 3rd 11 cm (4½ in) up from cast on edge and 6 more evenly spaced allowing for a 10th button in the neck edge.

Right side
Work the same as left side working buttonholes to correspond to button positions. Leave the 11 sts on a s.st.h.

Shoulder seam
Work 2 the same. With 3¼ mm (10) needles put 39 (42: 45: 48) sts from the back and the same from the front on to spare needles. Place these 2 needles side by side with the wrong sides of work facing each other. Then working on the right side of work, k tog a st from each needle to give 1 st on right hand needle. *K tog the next 2 sts (now 2 sts on right hand needle) then pass the 1st of these 2 sts over the 2nd. Repeat from * to work the rest of the sts.

Neck edge
With right side facing and 2¾ mm (12) needles start at right front border. Rib 11 sts from s.st.h for border, k across 8 (9: 10: 11) sts on s.st.h (right front), pick up and k 32 sts up side front, 1 st from shoulder seam, 3 sts down side back, 45 (47: 49: 51) sts on s.st.h (back neck edge), 3 sts up side back, 1 st from shoulder seam, 32 sts down side front, 8 (9: 10: 11) sts on s.st.h (left front) and rib across 11 sts of left front

border. (155: 159: 163: 167) sts. Work 9 rows in k1, p1 twisted rib working a buttonhole on the 4th row. Cast off loosely in rib.

Pocket top
With 2¾ mm (12) needles pick up and k the 20 sts on s.st.h then work 9 rows in k1, p1 twisted rib. Cast off loosely in rib.

SLEEVES
Work 2 the same. With right side facing and 3¼ mm (10) needles pick up and k 7 sts from s.st.h (armhole shaping), 103 (111: 119: 127) sts evenly along armhole edge with centre st at shoulder seam and 7 sts from s.st.h. (117: 125: 133: 141) sts. Continue in st.st dec 1 st at each end of 4th and every following 5th row as follows:

on k rows: k2, sl.1, k1, psso, k to last 4 sts, k2 tog, k2.

on p rows: p2, p2 tog, p to last 4 sts, p2 tog tbl, p2

until 57 (63: 69: 77) sts remain and sleeve measures 44 (45: 46: 46) cm 17 (17½: 18: 18) in. Change to 2¾ mm (12) needles and work 11 cm (4½ in) in k1, p1 twisted rib. Cast off loosely in rib.

MAKING UP
Work in all ends, sew borders to fronts working ease in evenly, sew side and sleeve seams, pocket top edges to front, pocket lining to inside of front and buttons to button positions as marked.

CLASSIC JUMPER
Ladies jumper in 4 ply wool

A very feminine jumper, fully fashioned and knitted in stocking stitch with a deep welt and collar in twisted rib. It can be worn as a twinset with the Classic Cardigan and can have long or short sleeves. It has the advantage of a true classic, looking either very country or very dressy depending on your accessories.

MATERIALS
Long sleeves
8 (9: 9: 10) 50 gm balls 4 ply wool
Short sleeves
6 (7: 7: 8) 50 gm balls 4 ply wool
2 2¾ mm (12) needles
2 3¼ mm (10) needles
4 2¾ mm (12) double pointed needles
4 3¼ mm (10) double pointed needles
stitch holders

MEASUREMENTS
Bust
86 (91: 97: 102) cm
34 (36: 38: 40) in
Actual measurement
94 (99: 104: 109) cm
37 (39: 41: 43) in
Finished length to shoulder
57 (58: 59: 60) cm
22½ (23: 23½: 24) in
Long sleeves
52 (53: 54: 54) cm
20½ (21: 21½: 21½) in
Short sleeves
20 (20: 20: 20) cm
8 (8: 8: 8) in

TENSION
28 sts and 36 rows for a 10 cm (4 in) square worked in st.st on 3¼ mm (10) needles

BACK
*With 2¾ mm (12) needles cast on 109 (117: 125: 133) sts. Work 11 cm (4½ in) in k1, p1 twisted rib (k into back of k sts). Change to 3¼

mm (10) needles and continue in st.st inc 1 st at each end of 5th and every following 10th row as follows:
k2, inc into next st, k to last 4 sts, inc into next st, k3
until there are 129 (137: 145: 153) sts. Work a further 7 rows. Work should measure about 39 cm (15½ in) from cast on edge.
Shape armholes
With right side facing k 7 sts at the beginning of next 2 rows and then put them on to s.st.h. (115: 123: 131: 139) sts.* Continue straight for 62 (66: 70: 74) rows. Leave all sts on a s.st.h for shoulder seams (36: 39: 42: 45) sts for each shoulder seam and (43: 45: 47: 49) sts for back neck edge.

FRONT
Work the same as Back from * to *. Continue straight for 30 (34: 38: 42) rows.
Shape neck
With right side facing
next row: k 46 (49: 52: 55) sts, turn and continue on these sts.
1st row: p2, p2 tog, p to end of row.
2nd row: k to last 4 sts, k2 tog, k2.
Repeat these last 2 rows until 36 (39: 42: 45) sts remain. Continue straight for 21 rows or until the front length corresponds to the back length. Leave sts on s.st.h for shoulder seam. Leave next 23 (25: 27: 29) sts on a s.st.h for front neck edge. Rejoin yarn to remaining 46 (49: 52: 55) sts and work the other side of front to match, working dec rows as follows:
1st row: p to last 4 sts, p2 tog tb1, p2.
2nd row: k2, sl.1, k1, psso, k to end of row.

Shoulder seam

Work 2 the same. With 3¼ mm (10) needles put 36 (39: 42: 45) sts from the back and the same from the front on to spare needles. Place these 2 needles side by side with the wrong sides of work facing each other. Then working on the right side of work, k tog a st from each needle to give 1 st on right hand needle. *K tog

end of every 6th row as follows:
k2, sl.1, k1, psso, k to last 4 sts, k2 tog, k2
until 65 (71: 77: 85) sts remain.

Shape cuff

next row: dec 8 (8: 10: 16) sts evenly across the row. (57: 63: 67: 69) sts. Change to 2¾ mm (12) needles and work 11 cm (4½ in) in k1, p1 twisted rib. Cast off loosely in rib.

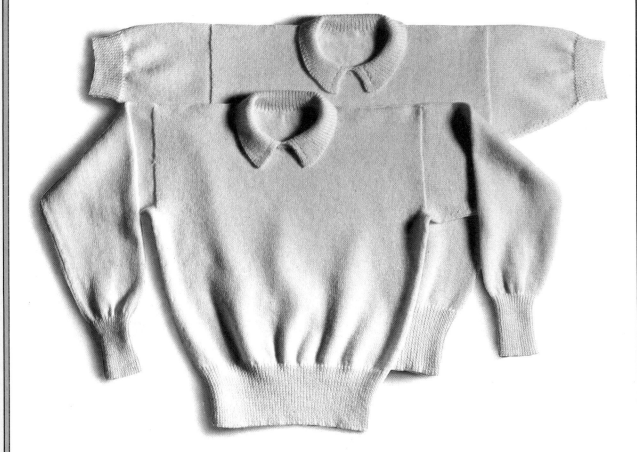

the next 2 sts (now 2 sts on right hand needle) then pass the 1st of these 2 sts over the 2nd. Repeat from * to work the rest of the sts.

Long sleeves

Work 2 the same. *With right side facing and 3¼ mm (10) needles pick up and k 7 sts on s.st.h (armhole shaping), 99 (107: 115: 123) sts evenly along armhole edge (centre st at shoulder seam) and 7 sts on s.st.h (113: 121: 129: 137) sts.* Continue in st.st dec 1 st at each

Short sleeves

Work the same as for long sleeves from * to *. Continue in st.st dec 1 st at each end of every 3rd row as follows:

on k rows: k2, sl.1, k1, psso, k to last 4 sts, k2 tog, k2.

on p rows: p2, p2 tog, p to last 4 sts, p2 tog tbl, p2.

until 77 (85: 93: 101) sts remain. Change to 2¾ mm (12) needles and work 5 cm (2 in) in k1, p1

twisted rib. Cast off loosely in rib.

Neck edge and collar

With right side facing and 4 2¾ mm (12) double pointed needles begin at centre front. Pick up and k 12 (13: 14: 15) sts from s.st.h (front neck edge), 28 sts up side front, 1 st from shoulder seam, 43 (45: 47: 49) sts from s.st.h (back neck edge), 1 st from shoulder seam, 27 sts down side front and remaining 11 (12: 13: 14) sts from s.st.h (front neck edge). (123: 127: 131: 135) sts. Work 7 rounds in k1, p1 rib, with alternate rounds in k1, p1 twisted rib (the two centre sts should both be k sts). Now divide for collar. Change to 4 3¼ mm (10) double pointed needles, turn and work in rows in k1, p1 twisted rib as follows:

1st row: k1, *k1, p1; repeat from * to last st, k1.
2nd row: (k1, p1) twice, inc into next st, rib to last 6 sts, inc into next st, rib to end of row.
3rd row: k2, p1, k1, p2, rib to last 6 sts, p2, k1, p1, k2.
4th row: as 2nd row.

Continue repeating these 4 rows until collar measures 5 cm (2 in) from the beg of the 4 row repeat. Work 2 more rows without inc. Cast off loosely in rib.

MAKING UP

Work in all ends of yarn, sew side and sleeve seams. Work a neat oversew strengthening st at the inside of centre front neck where collar divides.

TENNIS
Ladies cardigan in 4 ply wool

As long as a sunny day at Wimbledon, this is the ultimate cardigan. Totally simple and utterly practical, it is knitted in stocking stitch and fully fashioned, with a low round neck and two useful low set pockets finished in twisted rib. It can be dressed to look sporty or elegant depending on your mood.

MATERIALS
10 (11: 11: 12) 50 gm balls 4 ply wool
2 2¾ mm (12) needles
2 3¼ mm (10) needles
stitch holders
10 buttons 1.5 cm (½ in) diameter

MEASUREMENTS
Bust
86 (91: 97: 102) cm
34 (36: 38: 40) in
Measurement at widest point
97 (102: 107: 112) cm
38 (40: 42: 44) in
Finished length to shoulder
70 (71: 72: 73) cm
27½ (28: 28½: 29) in
Sleeve length
51 (52: 52: 53) cm
20 (20½: 20½: 21) in

TENSION
28 sts and 36 rows for a 10 cm (4 in) square worked in st.st on 3¼ mm (10) needles.

BACK
With 2¾ mm (12) needles cast on 135 (143: 151: 159) sts. Work 9 cm (3½ in) in k1, p1 twisted rib (k into back of k sts). Change to 3¼ mm (10) needles and continue in st.st. Work straight until work measures 46 cm (18 in) from cast on edge.
Shape armholes
With right side facing k 9 sts and put them on a s.st.h, k to last 9 sts and put these on a s.st.h. Turn and continue on remaining 117 (125: 133: 141) sts. Continue straight on these sts for 75

(79: 83: 87) rows.
Shape neck
With right side facing
next row: k49 (52: 55: 58) sts, turn, and continue on these sts.
1st row: p2, p2 tog, p to end of row.
2nd row: k to last 4 sts, k2 tog, k2.
Repeat these last 2 rows until 36 (39: 42: 45) sts remain. Leave these sts on a s.st.h for shoulder seam. Leave next 19 (21: 23: 25) sts on a s.st.h for back neck edge. Rejoin wool and continue on remaining 49 (52: 55: 58) sts, k to end of row. Now work other side of back to match working dec rows as follows:
1st row: p to last 4 sts, p2 tog tbl, p2.
2nd row: k2, sl.1, k1, psso, k to end of row.
Pocket linings
Work 2 the same. With 3¼ mm (10) needles cast on 35 sts, work 48 rows in st.st. Leave sts on a s.st.h.

LEFT FRONT
With 2¾ mm (12) needles cast on 73 (77: 81: 85) sts. Work in k1, p1 twisted rib working a k st at all edges and starting 1st row thus:
1st row: k2, *p1, k1; repeat from * to last st, k1.
2nd row: *k1, p1; repeat from * to last st, k1.
Continue repeating these 2 rows until rib measures 9 cm (3½ in). Change to 3¼ mm (10) needles and continue in st.st.
next row: k to last 9 sts, put these on a s.st.h (for front border), turn, and continue on remaining 64 (68: 72: 76) sts. Work straight for 47 rows.
Place pocket lining
With right side facing k7, slip next 35 sts on to a s.st.h and in place of these sts, k across the 35

sts of pocket lining, k to end of row. Continue straight until work measures 46 cm (18 in) from start and corresponds to back length measurement.

Shape armhole

With right side facing

next row: k 9 sts and put them on a s.st.h and continue on remaining 55 (59: 63: 67) sts.

must correspond to back length). Leave sts on a s.st.h (for shoulder seam).

To make a buttonhole

With right side facing k2, p1, k1, yfwd, k2 tog, work to end of row.

RIGHT FRONT

Work the same as left front, reversing all

Continue straight for 45 (49: 53: 57) rows.

Shape neck

With right side facing

next row: k to last 8 (9: 10: 11) sts, put these on a s.st.h and continue on remaining 47 (50: 53: 56) sts.

1st row: p.

2nd row: k to last 4 sts, k2 tog, k2.

Repeat these last 2 rows until 36 (39: 42: 45) sts remain. Continue straight for 22 rows (work

shapings and *pocket position* and working 2 buttonholes into the ribbing, the 1st 1 cm (½ in), the 2nd 6 cm (2½ in) up from cast on edge. Work neck dec row thus:

k2, sl.1, k1, psso, k to end of row.

Shoulder seam

Work 2 the same. With 3¼ mm (10) needles put 36 (39: 42: 45) sts from the back and the same from the front on to spare needles. Place these 2 needles side by side with the wrong sides of work facing each other. Then working on the right side of work, k tog a st from each needle to give 1 st on right hand needle. *K tog the next 2 sts (now 2 sts on right hand needle) then pass the 1st of these 2 sts over the 2nd. Repeat from * to work the rest of the sts.

FRONT BORDERS
Left side
With 2¾ mm (12) needles, pick up the 9 sts on s.st.h and work in k1, p1 twisted rib working a k st at all edges. Continue until border measures 5 cm (2 in) less than the front edge. Leave the 9 sts on a s.st.h. Mark the button positions, the 1st 1 cm (½ in), the 2nd 6 cm (2½ in) up from cast on edge and 7 more, evenly spaced, allowing for a 10th button in neck edge.
Right side
Work the same as left side working buttonholes to correspond to button positions.
Neck edge
With right side facing and 2¾ mm (12) needles start at right front border. Rib 9 sts from s.st.h, k across 8 (9: 10: 11) sts on s.st.h, pick up and k 41 sts up side front, 1 st at shoulder seam, 12 sts down side back, across 19 (21: 23: 25) sts on s.st.h (back neck edge), 12 sts up side back, 1 st at shoulder seam, 41 sts down side front, 8 (9: 10: 11) sts on s.st.h and rib across 9 sts of left front border. (161: 165: 169: 173) sts. Work

9 rows in k1, p1 twisted rib working a buttonhole on the 4th row. Cast off loosely in rib.
Pocket tops
Work 2 the same. With 2¾ mm (12) needles pick up and k the 35 sts on s.st.h and work 9 rows in k1, p1 twisted rib. Cast off loosely in rib.

SLEEVES
Work 2 the same. With right side facing and 3¼ mm (10) needles pick up and k 9 sts on s.st.h (armhole shaping), 131 (139: 147: 155) sts evenly along armhole edge, (centre st at shoulder seam) and 9 sts on s.st.h. (149: 157: 165: 173) sts. Now dec 1 st at each end of the 2nd and every following 4th row as follows: k2, sl.1, k1, psso, k to last 4 sts, k2 tog, k2. until 75 (81: 89: 95) sts remain.
Shape cuff
With wrong side facing
next row: dec 17 (19: 23: 25) sts evenly along row. (58: 62: 66: 70) sts. Change to 2¾ mm (12) needles and work 9 cm (3½ in) in k1, p1 twisted rib. Cast off loosely in rib.

MAKING UP
Work in all ends. Sew borders to fronts working the ease in equally, the buttons to button band as marked, side seams throughout, pocket linings to insides of fronts and pocket top edges to fronts.

SQUASH
Ladies waistcoat in 4 ply wool

This fully fashioned waistcoat is extra long. Starting in twisted rib, which is also used for the front borders and pocket tops, it goes on a very long way in stocking stitch. The armholes are cut deep intentionally for big shirt sleeves and the neck is scooped to make room for a tie should you so choose.

MATERIALS
7 (7: 8: 8) 50 gm balls 4 ply wool
2 2¾ mm (12) needles
2 3¼ mm (10) needles
4 2¾ mm (12) double pointed needles or circular needle
stitch holders
10 buttons 1.5 cm (½ in) diameter

MEASUREMENTS
Bust
86 (91: 97: 102) cm
34 (36: 38: 40) in
Measurement at widest point
99 (104: 109: 114) cm
39 (41: 43: 45) in
Finished length to shoulder
70 (71: 72: 73) cm
27½ (28: 28½: 29) in

TENSION
28 sts and 36 rows for a 10 cm (4 in) square worked in st.st on 3¼ mm (10) needles

BACK
With 2¾ mm (12) needles cast on 135 (143: 151: 159) sts. Work 9 cm (3½ in) in k1, p1 twisted rib (k into back of k sts). Change to 3¼ mm (10) needles and continue in st.st. Work straight until work measures 43 cm (17 in) from cast on edge.
Shape armholes
With right side facing work 7 sts at the beginning of the next 2 rows and put these sts on s.st.h (121: 129: 137: 145) sts. Now dec 1 st at each end of the next row as follows:
k2, sl.1, k1, psso, k to last 4 sts, k2 tog, k2.

next row: p.
Repeat the last 2 rows until 103 (111: 119: 127) sts remain. Continue straight for 60 (64: 68: 72) rows.
Shape neck
With right side facing
next row: k42 (45: 48: 51) sts, turn and continue on these sts.
1st row: p2, p2 tog, p to end of row.
2nd row: k to last 4 sts, k2 tog, k2.
Repeat these last 2 rows until 29 (32: 35: 38) sts remain. Leave these sts on a s.st.h for shoulder seam. Leave centre 19 (21: 23: 25) sts on a s.st.h for back neck edge. Rejoin wool and continue on remaining 42 (45: 48: 51) sts, k to end of row. Work to match other side working dec rows as follows:
1st row: p to last 4 sts, p2 tog tbl, p2.
2nd row: k2, sl.1, k1, psso, k to end of row.
Pocket linings
Work 2 the same. With 3¼ mm (10) needles cast on 35 sts. Work 50 rows in st.st. Leave sts on a s.st.h.

LEFT FRONT
With 2¾ mm (12) needles cast on 73 (77: 81: 85) sts. Work in k1, p1 twisted rib working a k st at all edges starting 1st row thus:
1st row: k2, *p1, k1; repeat from * to last st, k1.
Continue until rib measures 9 cm (3½ in). Change to 3¼ mm (10) needles and continue in st.st.
next row: k to last 9 sts, put these on a s.st.h (front border), turn and continue on remaining 64 (68: 72: 76) sts. Work straight for 50 rows.
Place pocket lining
With right side facing k7, slip next 35 sts on to a

s.st.h and in place of these k across the 35 sts of pocket lining, k to end of row. Continue straight until work measures 43 cm (17 in) and corresponds to back length.

Shape armhole

With right side facing k first 7 sts and put these sts on a s.st.h, k to end of row. Work 1 row p. Now dec 1 st at armhole edge as follows: k2, sl.1, k1, psso, k to end of row.

remain. Continue straight for 22 rows or until work corresponds to back length.

To make a buttonhole

With right side facing k2, p1, k1, yfwd, k2 tog, work to end of row.

RIGHT FRONT

Work the same as left reversing all shapings and *pocket position* while working 2

next row: p.

Repeat these 2 rows until 48 (52: 56: 60) sts remain. Continue straight for 28 (32: 36: 40) rows.

Shape neck

With right side facing

next row: k to last 8 (9: 10: 11) sts and put these on a s.st.h, turn and continue on remaining 40 (43: 46: 49) sts.

next row: p.

next row: k to last 4 sts, k2 tog, k2.

Repeat these last 2 rows until 29 (32: 35: 38) sts

buttonholes into the rib, the 1st 1 cm (½ in), the 2nd 6 cm (2½ in) up from cast on edge.

Work armhole dec row as follows:

k to last 4 sts, k2 tog, k2.

Work neck dec row as follows:

k2, sl.1, k1, psso, k to end of row.

Shoulder seam

Work 2 the same. With 3¼ mm (10) needles put 29 (32: 35: 38) sts from the back and the same from the front on to spare needles. Place these 2 needles side by side with the wrong sides of work facing each other. Then working on the right side of work k tog a st from each needle to give 1 st on right hand needle. *K tog the next 2 sts (now 2 sts on right hand needle) then pass the 1st of these 2 sts over the 2nd. Repeat from * to work the rest of the sts.

FRONT BORDERS
Left side
With 2¾ mm (12) needles pick up the 9 sts on s.st.h and work in k1, p1 twisted rib working a k st at all edges. Continue until border measures 5 cm (2 in) less than front edge. Leave the 9 sts on a s.st.h. Mark the button positions, the first 1 cm (½ in) the second 6 cm (2½ in) up from cast on edge and 7 more evenly spaced allowing for a 10th button in the neck edge.

Right side
Work the same as left, working buttonholes to correspond to button positions.

Neck edge
With right side facing and 2¾ mm (12) needles, start at right front border. Rib 9 sts on s.st.h, k8 (9: 10: 11) sts on s.st.h, pick up and k 41 sts up side front, 1 st at shoulder seam, 12 sts down side back, 19 (21: 23: 25) sts on s.st.h (back neck edge), 12 sts up side back, 1 st at shoulder seam, 41 sts down side front, 8 (9: 10: 11) sts on s.st.h and rib 9 sts from left front border. (161: 165: 169: 173) sts. Work 9 rows in k1, p1 twisted rib working a buttonhole on 4th row. Cast off in rib.

Pocket tops
Work 2 the same. With 2¾ mm (12) needles pick up and k the 35 sts on s.st.h and work 9 rows in k1, p1 twisted rib. Cast off loosely in rib.

Armhole edges
Work 2 the same. With right side facing and 4 2¾ mm (12) double pointed needles or circular needle pick up and k 7 sts from s.st.h, 168 (176: 184: 192) sts evenly around armhole edge with centre at shoulder seam, 7 sts from s.st.h. (182: 190: 198: 206) sts. Divide evenly on to 3 needles and work 9 rounds in k1, p1 rib (every other round in twisted rib). Cast off in rib so that edge is neither pulled or splayed out.

MAKING UP
Work in all ends, sew borders to fronts working the ease in equally, buttons to button band as marked, pocket linings to inside of fronts, pocket top edges to fronts and through side seams.

BETH
Ladies sweater in 4 ply wool

A thoroughbred version of the school sweater, this has the distinction of a long, long line and a deep scoop at the neck. The sweater is knitted in stocking stitch and fully fashioned while the collar and tops of the low set pockets are in rib.

MATERIALS
10 (11: 11: 12) 50 gm balls 4 ply wool
2 2¾ mm (12) needles
2 3¼ mm (10) needles
4 2¾ mm (12) double pointed needles
4 3¼ mm (10) double pointed needles
stitch holders

MEASUREMENTS
Bust
86 (91: 97: 102) cm
34 (36: 38: 40) in
Actual measurement
97 (102: 107: 112) cm
38 (40: 42: 44) in
Finished length to shoulder
70 (71: 72: 73) cm
27½ (28: 28½: 29) in
Sleeve length
51 (52: 52: 53) cm
20 (20½: 20½: 21) in

TENSION
28 sts and 36 rows for a 10 cm (4 in) square worked in st.st on 3¼ mm (10) needles

BACK
*With 2¾ mm (12) needles cast on 134 (142: 150: 158) sts. Work 9 cm (3½ in) in k2, p2 rib, increasing 1 st at the end of the last row. (135: 143: 151: 159) sts. Change to 3¼ mm (10) needles and continue in st.st * until work measures 46 cm (18 in) from cast on edge.
Shape armholes
With right side facing
next row: k the first 9 sts and put them on s.st.h, k to last 9 sts and put these on a s.st.h. Turn work and continue on remaining 117 (125:

133: 141) sts. Work straight for 87 (91: 95: 99) rows. Leave all sts on a s.st.h for shoulder seams and back neck.
Pocket linings
Work 2 the same. With 3¼ mm (10) needles cast on 35 sts, and work 46 rows in st.st. Leave all sts on a s.st.h.

FRONT
Work the same as Back from * to * until 46 rows have been worked in st.st.
Place pocket linings
With right side facing k7, slip next 35 sts on to a s.st.h and in place of these, k across 35 sts of pocket lining, k 51 (59: 67: 75) sts, sl. next 35 sts on to a s.st.h and in place of these k across 35 sts of pocket lining, k7. Continue straight until work measures 46 cm (18 in) and corresponds to back length.
Shape armholes
With right side facing
next row: k the first 9 sts and put them on a s.st.h, k to last 9 sts and put these on a s.st.h. Turn and continue on remaining 117 (125: 133: 141) sts. Work straight for 43 (47: 51: 55) rows.
Shape neck
With right side facing
next row: k 49 (52: 55: 58) sts, turn and continue on these sts.
1st row: p.
2nd row: k to last 4 sts, k2 tog, k2.
Repeat these last 2 rows until 38 (41: 44: 47) sts remain. Work straight until front corresponds to back length (20 rows). Leave sts on a s.st.h for shoulder seam. Leave next 19 (21: 23: 25) sts on a s.st.h for front neck edge, rejoin wool to remaining 49 (52: 55: 58) sts, k to end of row. Now work the other side of front to match,

working dec. row as follows:

2nd row: k2, sl.1, k1, psso, k to end of row.

Shoulder seam

Work 2 the same. With 3¼ mm (10) needles put 38 (41: 44: 47) sts from the back and the same from the front on to spare needles. Place these 2 needles side by side with the wrong

seam, 41 (43: 45: 47) sts from s.st.h (back neck edge), 1 st from shoulder seam, 42 sts down side front and the remaining 9 (10: 11: 12) sts from s.st.h. (145: 149: 153: 157) sts. Starting at centre front, work 10 rounds in k1, p1 rib (the two centre front sts should both be k sts). Now divide for collar. Change to 4 3¼ mm (10)

sides of work facing each other. Then working on the right side of work, k tog a st from each needle to give 1 st on right hand needle. *K tog the next 2 sts (now 2 sts on right hand needle) then pass the 1st of these 2 sts over the 2nd. Repeat from * to work the rest of the sts.

Neck edge and collar

With right side facing, start at centre front. With 4 2¾ mm (12) double pointed needles pick up and k 10 (11: 12: 13) sts from s.st.h (front neck edge), 41 sts up side front, 1 st from shoulder

double pointed needles, turn, and work in rows as follows:

1st row: k1, *k1, p1; repeat from * to last st, k1.

2nd row: (k1, p1) twice, inc into next st, rib to last 6 sts, inc into next st, rib to end of row.

3rd row: k2, p1, k1, p2, rib to last 6 sts, p2, k1, p1, k2.

4th row: as 2nd row.

Continue repeating these 4 rows until collar measures 8 cm (3 in) from the beginning of the 4 row repeat. Work 2 more rows without inc.

Cast off loosely in rib.
Pocket tops
Work 2 the same. With 2¾ mm (12) needles pick up and k the 35 sts on s.st.h. Work 9 rows in k1, p1 rib. Cast off loosely in rib.

SLEEVES
Work 2 the same. With right side facing and 3¼ mm (10) needles, pick up and k9 sts on s.st.h (armhole shaping), 131 (139: 147: 155) sts evenly along armhole edge with centre st at shoulder seam and 9 sts on s.st.h (armhole shaping). (149: 157: 165: 173) sts. Now dec 1 st at each end of 2nd and every following 4th row as follows:

k2, sl.1, k1, psso, k to last 4 sts, k2 tog, k2 until 75 (81: 89: 95) sts remain.
Shape cuff
With wrong side facing
next row: dec 17 (19: 23: 25) sts evenly along row. (58: 62: 66: 70) sts. Change to 2¾ mm (12) needles and work 9 cm (3½ in) in k2, p2 rib. Cast off loosely in rib.

MAKING UP
Work in all ends of yarn, sew pocket linings to inside of front, pocket edges to front, side and sleeve seams and work a neat oversew strengthening st at the inside of centre front neck where the collar divides.

ZIGGY

Teenage and ladies jumper in 4 ply wool

Inspired by traditional Guernsey designs, this sweater uses three different stitches for greater effect. The zig-zags and diamonds are in moss stitch, the ribs in reverse stocking stitch and the collar is knitted in garter stitch. The same rib defines the head of the sleeves.

MATERIALS

9 (11) 50 gm balls 4 ply wool
2 2¾ mm (12 needles)
2 3 mm (11) needles
2 3¼ mm (10) needles
4 2¾ mm (12) double pointed needles
stitch holders

MEASUREMENTS

Bust
teenage 76-81 cm (30-32 in)
ladies 91-97 cm (36-38 in)
Measurement at widest point
94 (113) cm
37 (44½) in
Finished length to shoulder
63 (67) cm
25 (26½) in
Sleeve length
46 (50) cm
18 (19½) in

TENSION

28 sts and 36 rows for a 10 cm (4 in) square worked in st.st on 3¼ mm (10) needles

BACK AND FRONT

Both the same. With 2¾ mm (12) needles cast on 104 (126) sts and work 9 cm (3½ in) in k2, p2 rib. Change to 3¼ mm (10) needles.
next row: inc 27 (31) sts evenly across the row. (131: 157) sts. Now continue in st.st until work measures 25 (29) cm, 10 (11½) in from cast on edge.
Now work in Zig Zag pattern as follows with right side facing
1st row: 0 (p1, k12), *k13, p1, k12; repeat from

* to last 1 (14) sts, k1 (k13, p1).
2nd row: p1 (p1, k1, p12), *p11, k1, p1, k1, p12; repeat from * to last 0 (13) sts, 0 (p11, k1, p1).
3rd row: 0 (k2, p1, k10), *k11, p1, k3, p1, k10; repeat from * to last 1 (14) sts, k1 (k11, p1, k2).
4th row: p1 (k1, p2, k1, p10), *p9, (k1, p2) twice, k1, p10; repeat from * to last 0 (13) sts, 0 (p9, k1, p2, k1).
5th row: 0 (k1, p1, k2, p1, k8), *k9, p1, k2, p1, k1, p1, k2, p1, k8; repeat from * to last 1 (14) sts, k1 (k9, p1, k2, p1, k1).
6th row: p1 [(p2, k1) twice, p8], *p7, k1, p2, k1, p3, k1, p2, k1, p8; repeat from * to last 0 (13) sts, 0 [p7, (k1, p2) twice].
7th row: 0 [(p1, k2) twice, p1, k6], *k7, (p1, k2) 4 times, p1, k6; repeat from * to last 1 (14) sts, k1 [k7, (p1, k2) twice, p1].
8th row: p1 [p1, k1, (p2, k1) twice, p6], *p5, (k1, p2) twice, k1, p1, (k1, p2) twice, k1, p6; repeat from * to last 0 (13) sts, work 0 [p5, (k1, p2) twice, k1, p1].
9th row: 0 [(k2, p1) 3 times, k4], *k5, (p1, k2) twice, p1, k3, (p1, k2) twice, p1, k4; repeat from * to last 1 (14) sts, k1 [k5, (p1, k2) 3 times].
10th row: p1 [p3, (k1, p2) twice, k1, p4], *p3, (k1, p2) twice, k1, p5, (k1, p2) twice, k1, p4; repeat from * to last 0 (13) sts, 0 [p3, (k1, p2) 3 times, p1].
11th row: 0 [k4, (p1, k2) 3 times], *k3, (p1, k2) twice, p1, k7, (p1, k2) 3 times; repeat from * to last 1 (14) sts, k1 [k3, (p1, k2) 3 times, k2].
12th row: p1 [p5, (k1, p2) 3 times], *p1, (k1, p2) twice, k1, p9, (k1, p2) 3 times; repeat from * to last 0 (13) sts, 0 [p1, (k1, p2) 3 times, p3].
13th row: 0 [k6, (p1, k2) twice, p1], *k1, (p1, k2) twice, p1, k11, (p1, k2) twice, p1; repeat

from * to last 1 (14) sts, k1 [k1, (p1, k2) 3 times, k4].

14th row: k1 [p7, (k1, p2) twice, k1], *(p2, k1) twice, p13, (k1, p2) twice, k1; repeat from * to last 0 (13) sts, 0 [(p2, k1) twice, p7].

15th row: 0 (k8, p1, k2, p1, k1), * (k2, p1) twice, k15, p1, k2, p1, k1; repeat from * to last 1 (14) sts, k1 [(k2, p1) twice, k8].

16th row: p1 (p9, k1, p2, k1, p1), *k1, p2, k1, p17, k1, p2, k1, p1; repeat from * to last 0 (13) sts, 0 (k1, p2, k1, p9).

17th row: 0 (k10, p1, k2), *p1, k2, p1, k19, p1, k2; repeat from * to last 1 (14) sts, p1 (p1, k2, p1, k10).

18th row: p1 (p11, k1, p2), *p1, k1, p21, k1, p2; repeat from * to last 0 (13) sts, 0 (p1, k1, p11).

19th row: 0 (k12, p1), *k1, p1, k23, p1; repeat from * to last 1 (14) sts, k1 (k1, p1, k12).

20th row: k1, (p13, k1), *p25, k1; repeat from * to last 0 (13) sts, 0 (p13).

These 20 rows make 1 Zig Zag pattern. Repeat 4 more times. Now begin Diamond Pattern as follows:

1st row: 0 (p1, k12), *k13, p1, k12; repeat from* to last 1 (14) sts, k1 (k13, p1).

2nd row: p1 (p1, k1, p12), *p11, k1, p1, k1, p12; repeat from * to last 0 (13) sts, 0 (p11, k1, p1).

3rd row: 0 (p1, k1, p1, k10), *k11, (p1, k1) twice, p1, k10; repeat from * to last 1 (14) sts, k1 (k11, p1, k1, p1).

4th row: p1 [(p1, k1) twice, p10], *p9, (k1, p1) 3 times, k1, p10; repeat from * to last 0 (13) sts, 0 [p9, (k1, p1) twice].

5th row: 0 [(p1, k1) twice, p1, k8], *k9, (p1, k1) 4 times, p1, k8; repeat from * to last 1 (14) sts, k1 [k9, (p1, k1) twice, p1].

6th row: p1 [(p1, k1) 3 times, p8], *p7, (k1, p1) 5 times, k1, p8; repeat from * to last 0 (13) sts, 0 [p7, (k1, p1) 3 times].

7th row: 0 [(p1, k1) 3 times, p1, k6], *k7, (p1, k1) 6 times, p1, k6; repeat from * to last 1 (14) sts, k1 [k7, (p1, k1) 3 times, p1].

8th row: p1 [(p1, k1) 4 times, p6] *p5, (k1, p1) 7 times, k1, p6; repeat from * to last 0 (13) sts, 0 [p5, (k1, p1) 4 times].

9th row: 0 [(p1, k1) 4 times, p1, k4], *k5 (p1, k1) 8 times, p1, k4; repeat from * to last 1 (14) sts, k1 [k5, (p1, k1) 4 times, p1].

10th row: p1 [(p1, k1) 5 times, p4], *p3, (k1, p1) 9 times, k1, p4; repeat from * to last 0 (13) sts, 0 [p3, (k1, p1) 5 times].

11th row: 0 [(p1, k1) 5 times, p1, k2], *k3, (p1, k1) 10 times, p1, k2; repeat from * to last 1 (14) sts, k1 [k3, (p1, k1) 5 times, p1].

12th row: p1 [(p1, k1) 6 times, p2], *(p1, k1) 12 times, p2; repeat from * to last 0 (13) sts, 0 [(p1, k1) 6 times, p1].

13th row: k1 (0), *p1, k1; repeat from * to last 0 (1) st, p1.

14th row: k1 (0), *p1, k1; repeat from * to last 0 (1) st, p1.

15th to 27th rows: work pattern backwards starting with 13th row and ending with 1st row. These 27 rows complete the diamond pattern. Now work 3 rows in st.st.

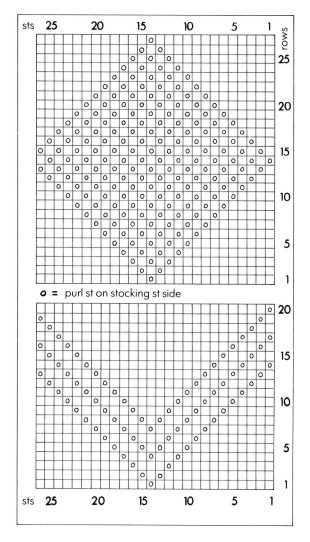

o = purl st on stocking st side

Graphs showing zigzag and diamond patterns

Shoulder ribs
Change to 3 mm (11) needles and with right side of work facing work 3 rows in r.st.st then 2 rows in st.st. Repeat these last 5 rows 3 more times making 4 bands of r.st.st in all. Leave all sts on a s.st.h for shoulder seam and collar.

Shoulder seams
Work 2 the same. With 3¼ mm (10) needles put 37 (46) sts from the back and the same from the front on to spare needles. Place these 2 needles side by side with the wrong sides of work facing each other. Then working on the right side of work k tog a st from each needle to give 1 st on right hand needle. *K tog the next 2 sts (now 2 sts on right hand needle) then pass the 1st of these 2 sts over the 2nd. Repeat from * to work rest of sts.

COLLAR
With right side facing and 4 2¾ mm (12) double pointed needles put the sts for the neck plus 1 st from each shoulder seam on 3 of the needles allowing for collar opening at centre front. 116 (132) sts. Work 10 rounds in k1, p1 rib starting at centre front. Now divide for collar at centre front and begin to work in rows. Turn and work in g.st until collar measures 9 cm (3½ in) from pick up row. With wrong side of collar facing cast off so that collar sits properly, and is not pulled in or splayed out.

SLEEVES
Work 2 the same. First count 88 (104) rows either side of shoulder seam for armhole depth. With right side facing and 3 mm (11) needles pick up and knit 109 (135) sts along this armhole edge (only 21 sts should go over shoulder ribs) and centre st on shoulder seam. Work 1 row p, then the next 3 rows in r.st.st. Change to 3¼ mm (10) needles and work 3 rows in st.st. Now work 1 pattern of Zig Zag pattern as given for front and back, starting 1st row as follows and *at the same time* keeping continuity of pattern correct, dec 1 st at each end of every 6th (5th) row.
1st row: k2, *k13, p1, k12; repeat from * to last 3 sts, k3. This sets position of pattern. When Zig Zag pattern is complete, continue in st.st and dec as set until 69 (79) sts remain and work measures 37 (41) cm 14½ (16) in from pick up edge.

Shape cuff
Dec 19 (23) sts evenly along next row to leave 50 (56) sts. Change to 2¾ mm (12) needles and work 9 cm (3½ in) in k2, p2 rib. Cast off loosely in rib.

MAKING UP
Work in all ends. Sew side and sleeve seams and work a neat strengthening st on inside of centre front neck edge where collar divides.

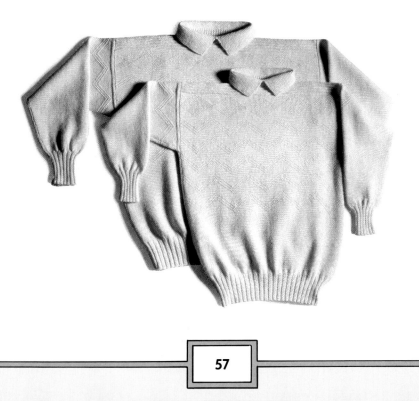

SOCCER
Man's sweater in double knit wool

A really sporty sweater with a shape that is based on a comfortable sweat shirt, chunky and knitted in stocking stitch. Two sturdy cables run from front to back and there is a ribbed V inset at the neck.

MATERIALS
13 (14: 15: 16) 50 gm balls double knit wool
2 3¼ mm (10) needles
2 4 mm (8) needles
4 3¼ mm (10) double pointed needles
cable needles
stitch holders

MEASUREMENTS
Chest
97 (102: 107: 112) cm
38 (40: 42: 44) in
Measurement at widest point
117 (123: 127: 132) cm
46 (48: 50: 52) in
Finished length to shoulder
69 (70: 71: 72) cm
27 (27½: 28: 28½) in
Sleeve length
56 (57: 58: 58) cm
22 (22½: 23: 23) in

TENSION
22 sts and 30 rows for a 10 cm (4 in) square worked in st.st on 4 mm (8) needles.

BACK
*With 3¼ mm (10) needles cast on 102 (108: 114: 120) sts and work 9 cm (3½ in) in k2, p2 rib. Change to 4 mm (8) needles and work as follows:
next row: k 16 (19: 22: 25) sts, *k1, inc into next st; repeat from * to last 16 (19: 22: 25) sts, k to end of row. (137: 143: 149: 155) sts.
next row: p.
now continue in pattern as follows:
1st row: k 17 (20: 23: 26) sts, p2, k4, p2, k10, p2, k4, p2, k51, p2, k4, p2, k10, p2, k4, p2, k to end of row.

2nd row: p 17 (20: 23: 26) sts, k2, p4, k2, p10, k2, p4, k2, p51, k2, p4, k2, p10, k2, p4, k2, p to end of row.
Repeat these last 2 rows 9 more times.
21st row: k 17 (20: 23: 26) sts, p2, k4, p2, cable next 10 sts (slip 1st 5 sts on to a cable needle and leave at front of work, k5, k5 from cable needle), p2, k4, p2, k51, p2, k4, p2, cable next 10 sts as before, p2, k4, p2, k to end of row.
22nd row: as 2nd row.
These last 22 rows make one pattern. Continue in pattern until work measures 43 cm (17 in) from cast on edge.
Shape armholes
With right side facing k 7 sts and leave on a s.st.h, work to last 7 sts and put these on a s.st.h, turn, and continue on remaining 123 (129: 135: 141) sts. *Continue straight for 61 (65: 69: 73) rows.
Shape neck
With right side facing
next row: work 46 (49: 52: 55) sts, turn, and continue on these sts.
1st row: p2, p2 tog, work to end of row.
2nd row: work to last 4 sts, k2 tog, k2.
Repeat these last 2 rows until 38 (41: 44: 47) sts remain. Work 5 more rows. Leave sts on a s.st.h for shoulder seam. Leave next 31 sts on a s.st.h for back neck. Rejoin yarn and continue on remaining 46 (49: 52: 55) sts. Work to end of row. Now work to match other side of back, reversing shaping and working dec rows as follows:
1st row: work to last 4 sts, p2 tog tbl, p2.
2nd row: k2, sl.1, k1, psso, work to end of row.

FRONT
Work the same as Back for * to *. Continue straight for 17 (21: 25: 29) rows.

Divide for front neck inset
With right side facing (*not fully fashioned*) work 61 (64: 67: 70) sts, turn and continue on these sts, dec 1 st at inset edge on every alternate row until 46 (49: 52: 55) sts remain. *Mark this row at neck edge on both sides*.

front on a s.st.h for front neck inset. Rejoin yarn and work remaining 61 (64: 67: 70) sts to match other side of front, reversing shaping and working neck shaping (*not inset edge*) as follows:
1st row: k2, sl.1, k1, psso, work to end of row.

Shape neck
With right side facing (*fully fashioned*)
1st row: Work to last 4 sts, k2 tog, k2.
2nd row: p2, p2 tog, work to end of row.
Repeat these last 2 rows until 38 (41: 44: 47) sts remain. Work straight for 18 rows. Leave sts on a s.st.h for shoulder seam. Leave centre st of

2nd row: work to last 4 sts, p2 tog tbl, p2.
Shoulder seam
Work 2 the same. With 4 mm (8) needles put 38 (41: 44: 47) sts from the back and the same from the front on to spare needles. Place these 2 needles side by side with the wrong sides of work facing each other. Then working on the

right side of work, k tog a st from each needle to give 1 st on right hand needle. *K tog the next 2 sts (now 2 sts on right hand needle) then pass the 1st of these 2 sts over the 2nd. Repeat from * to work rest of sts.

Front neck inset

With right side facing and 3¼ mm (10) needles pick up the st on s.st.h and work p1, k1, p1 into this stitch.

next row: inc into 1st st, p1, inc into last st.

next row: k1, p1, to last st, k1.

next row: inc into 1st st, k1, p1, k1, inc into last st.

Now continue in rib as set inc 1 st at each end of every alternate row until there are 31 sts. Work 2 more rows without inc, leave sts on s.st.h for front neck edge.

Neck edge

With right side facing and 4 3¼ mm (10) double pointed needles and starting at side front at neck shaping mark, pick up and k 20 sts up side front, 1 st at shoulder seam, 11 sts down side back, 31 sts from s.st.h (back neck edge), 11 sts up side back, 1 st at shoulder seam, 20 sts down side front and rib across 31 sts of front neck inset. (126 sts). Work 7 rounds in k1, p1 rib. Cast off *loosely* in rib. *Make sure a man will be able to get his head through*.

SLEEVES

Work 2 the same. With right side facing and 4 mm (8) needles pick up and k 7 sts from s.st.h (armhole shaping), 109 (115: 121: 127) sts evenly along armhole edge with centre stitch at shoulder seam and 7 sts from s.st.h (123: 129: 135: 141) sts. Continue in st.st and dec 1 st at each end of the 6th and every following 4th row as follows:

k2, sl.1, k1, psso, k to last 4 sts, k2 tog, k2 until 55 (59: 63: 69) sts remain.

Shape cuff

With wrong side facing

next row: dec 7 (9: 11: 15) sts evenly across row. (48: 50: 52: 54) sts.

Change to 3¼ mm (10) needles and work 9 cm (3½ in) in k2, p2 rib. Cast off loosely in rib.

MAKING UP

Work in all ends. Sew V inset into front neatly, sew side and sleeve seams.

SOPHIE
Ladies jumper in 4 ply wool

A decidedly dressy shape for the evening. From its deep twisted rib welt to its little rib collar, this jumper is patterned all over with delicate lacy flowers, each one centred with a bead.

MATERIALS
8 (9: 9: 10) 50 gm balls 4 ply wool
2 2¾ mm (12) needles
2 3¼ mm (10) needles
4 2¾ mm (12) double pointed needles
4 3¼ mm (10) double pointed needles
stitch holders
approx 900 (1000: 1000: 1100) beads with hole large enough to thread on to yarn

MEASUREMENTS
86 (91: 97: 102) cm
34 (36: 38: 40) in
Actual measurement
94 (99: 104: 109) cm
37 (39: 41: 43) in
Finished length to shoulder
57 (58: 59: 60) cm
22½ (23: 23½: 24) in
Sleeve length
50 (51: 52: 52) cm
19½ (20: 20½: 20½) in

TENSION
28 sts and 41 rows for a 10 cm (4 in) square worked in pattern on 3¼ mm (10) needles

BACK
**With 2¾ mm (12) needles cast on 109 (117: 125: 133) sts. Work 11 cm (4½ in) in k1, p1 twisted rib (k into back of k sts). Change to 3¼ mm (10) needles. Before starting to work pattern, thread approx 120 beads per ball (with a fine darning needle, thread wool on to needle and pass through hole in beads). Now continue in pattern as follows *at the same time* inc 1 st at each end of the 15th and every following 10th row. Work 2 rows in st.st.

1st row: k 0 (4: 2: 0) sts, *k5, yfwd, sl.1, k2 tog, psso, yfwd, k4; repeat from * to last 1 (5: 3: 1) sts, k 1 (5: 3: 1) sts.
2nd and following alternate rows: p.
3rd row: k0 (sl.1, k1, psso, k2: k2: k0) sts, *k3, k2 tog, yfwd, k1, k1 with bead, k1, yfwd, sl.1, k1, psso, k2; repeat from * to last 1 (5: 3: 1) sts, k 1 (5: 3: 1) sts.
5th row: repeat 1st row.
7th row: k.
9th row: k2 tog, yfwd, k9, yfwd, sl.1 (k3, yfwd, sl.1: k1, yfwd, sl.1: k2 tog, yfwd, k9, yfwd, sl.1) sts, *k2 tog, psso, yfwd, k9, yfwd, sl.1; repeat from * to last 13 (5: 3: 13) sts, k2 tog, psso, yfwd, k11 (k2 tog, psso, yfwd, k3: k2 tog, psso, yfwd, k1: k2 tog, psso, yfwd, k11).
11th row: k 0 (k1, k2 tog, yfwd, k1: k2: k0) sts, *k1 with bead, k1, yfwd, sl.1, k1, psso, k5; k2 tog, yfwd, k1; repeat from * to last 1 (5: 3: 1) sts, k1 (k1 with bead, k1, yfwd, sl.1, k1, psso, k1: k1 with bead, k2: k1).
13th row: repeat 9th row.
15th row: k.
16th row: p.

These last 16 rows make 1 pattern. Continue as set keeping continuity correct over inc and working pattern in when number of sts allow until there are 129 (137: 145: 153) sts. Work a further 8 rows. Work should measure approx 39 cm (15½ in) from cast on edge.

Shape armholes
With right side facing and keeping continuity of pattern correct, at the beg of next two rows work the 1st 7 sts and put them on s.st.h. (115: 123: 131: 139) sts.** Continue straight for 70 (74: 78: 82) rows. Leave all sts on a s.st.h for shoulder seams (36: 39: 42: 45) sts each and back neck edge (43: 45: 47: 49) sts.

FRONT

Work the same as Back from ** to **. Continue straight for 34 (38: 42: 46) rows.

Shape neck

With right side facing and keeping continuity of pattern correct,

next row: work 46 (49: 52: 55) sts, turn and continue on these sts dec 1 st at neck edge

same from the front on to spare needles. Place these 2 needles side by side with the wrong sides of work facing each other. Then working on right side of work k tog a st from each needle to give 1 st on right hand needle. *K tog the next 2 sts, now 2 sts on right hand needle, then pass the 1st of these 2 sts over the 2nd. Repeat from * to work rest of sts.

every row until 36 (39: 42: 45) sts remain. Continue straight for 25 rows and front corresponds to back length. Leave sts on s.st.h for shoulder seam, leave centre 23 (25: 27: 29) sts on a s.st.h for front neck edge. Rejoin yarn to remaining 46 (49: 52: 55) sts and work to match other side.

Shoulder seam

Work 2 the same. With 3¼ mm (10) needles put 36 (39: 42: 45) sts from the back and the

SLEEVES

Work 2 the same. With 3¼ mm (10) needles and right side facing, pick up and k 7 sts from s.st.h (armhole shaping) and 99 (107: 115: 123) sts evenly along armhole edge with centre stitch at shoulder seam, and 7 sts from s.st.h (113: 121: 129: 137) sts. Continue in pattern as given for back dec 1 st at each end of every 6th row and starting 1st row of pattern as follows:

1st row: k 2 (0: 4: 2) sts, *k5, yfwd, sl.1, k2 tog,

Close-up of stitch detail (actual size)

psso, yfwd, k4; repeat from * to last 3 (1: 5: 3) sts, k 3 (1: 5: 3) sts.
This sets the position of pattern. Continue as set until 63 (69: 75: 83) sts remain and work measures 39 (40: 41: 41) cm 15 (15½: 16: 16) in.

Shape cuff
With wrong side facing

next row: dec 6 (8: 10: 14) sts evenly along row. (57: 61: 65: 69) sts. Change to 2¾ mm (12) needles and work 11 cm (4½ in) in k1, p1 twisted rib. Cast off loosely in rib.

Neck edge and collar
With right side facing and 4 2¾ mm (12) double pointed needles, start at centre front. Pick up and k 12 (13: 14: 15) sts from s.st.h (front neck edge), 28 sts up side front, 1 st at shoulder seam, 43 (45: 47: 49) sts from s.st.h (back neck edge), 1 st at shoulder seam, 27 sts down side front and remaining 11 (12: 13: 14) sts from s.st.h (front neck edge). (123: 127: 131: 135) sts. Work 7 rounds in k1, p1 rib with every alternate round in k1, p1 twisted rib with the centre front sts both k sts. Divide for collar. Change to 4 3¼ mm (10) double pointed needles and work in rows. Starting at centre front, turn and work in k1, p1 twisted rib thus:
1st row: k1, *k1, p1; repeat from * to last st, k1.
2nd row: (k1, p1) twice, inc into next st, rib to last 6 sts, inc into next st, rib to end of row.
3rd row: k2, p1, k1, p2, rib to last 6 sts, p2, k1, p1, k2.
4th row: work as 2nd row.
Continue repeating these 4 rows until collar measures 5 cm (2 in) from beg of 4 row repeat. Work 2 more rows without inc. Cast off loosely in rib.

MAKING UP
Work in all ends. Sew side and sleeve seams. Work a neat strengthening stitch at the inside of centre front where collar divides.

OSCAR
Man's cardigan in 4 ply wool

This is a light-weight cardigan knitted in stocking stitch. It can have either a simple round neck or a collar — both of these are in twisted rib as is the rest of the detailing. The shape is short and waisted, perhaps more suitable for the relaxed atmosphere of the 'inn' than for the great outdoors.

MATERIALS
12 (13: 13: 14) 50 gm balls 4 ply wool
2 2¾ mm (12) needles
2 3¼ mm (10) needles
stitch holders
8 buttons 1.5 cm (½ in) diameter

MEASUREMENTS
Chest
97 (102: 107: 112) cm
38 (40: 42: 44) in
Measurement at widest point
114 (119: 124: 129) cm
45 (47: 49: 51) in
Finished length to shoulder
67 (68: 69: 70) cm
26½ (27: 27½: 28) in
Sleeve length
56 (57: 58: 58) cm
22 (22½: 23: 23) in

TENSION
28 sts and 36 rows for a 10 cm (4 in) square worked in st.st on 3¼ mm (10) needles

BACK
With 2¾ mm (12) needles cast on 130 (138: 146: 154) sts. Work 10 cm (4 in) in k1, p1 twisted rib (k into back of k sts). Change to 3¼ mm (10) needles and continue in st.st inc 1 st at each end of the 3rd and every following 4th row as follows:
With right side facing k2, inc into next st, k to last 4 sts, inc into next st, k3
until there are 158 (166: 174: 182) sts. Work straight until work measures 43 cm (17 in) from cast on edge.

Shape armholes
With right side facing k 9 sts and put these sts on a s.st.h, k to last 9 sts and put these on a s.st.h Turn and continue on remaining 140 (148: 156: 164) sts.
Round necked version
Continue straight for 81 (85: 89: 93) rows.
Shape neck
With right side facing
next row: k 49 (52: 55: 58) sts, turn and continue on these sts. Work 3 rows. Leave these sts on a s.st.h for shoulder seam, leave centre 42 (44: 46: 48) sts on a s.st.h for back neck edge. Rejoin wool and continue on remaining 49 (52: 55: 58) sts, k to end of row and work to match other side of back.
Version with collar
Continue straight for 85 (89: 93: 97) rows. Leave all sts on a s.st.h for shoulder seams and neck edge.
Pocket linings
Work 2 the same. With 3¼ mm (10) needles cast on 36 sts and work 40 rows in st.st. Leave sts on a s.st.h.
To make a buttonhole
With right side facing work to last 7 sts, yfwd, k2 tog, work to end of row.

LEFT FRONT
With 2¾ mm (12) needles cast on 71 (75: 79: 83) sts. Work in k1, p1 twisted rib working a k st at all edges and starting 1st row thus:
k2, *p1, k1; repeat from * to last st, k1.
Continue until rib measures 10 cm (4 in) *at the same time* working 2 buttonholes, the 1st 1 cm (½ in), the 2nd 9 cm (3½ in) from bottom edge. Change to 3¼ mm (10) needles.

next row: k to last 11 sts, put these on a s.st.h (for front border) turn, and continue on remaining 60 (64: 68: 72) sts. Continue in st.st inc 1 st at the beginning of the 3rd and every following 4th row as follows:
k2, inc into next st, k to end of row until there are 74 (78: 82: 86) sts. *At the same time* when 40 rows have been worked in st.st

Place pocket linings
With right side facing k 9 sts, slip next 36 sts on to a s.st.h and in place of these k across 36 sts of pocket lining, k to end of row. Continue straight until work measures 43 cm (17 in) from cast on edge and corresponds to back length.

Shape armhole
With right side facing k 9 sts and put these sts on a s.st.h. Continue on remaining 65 (69: 73: 77) sts. Work straight for 50 (54: 58: 62) rows.

Shape neck
With right side facing
next row: k to last 7 (8: 9: 10) sts, put these on a s.st.h, turn and continue on remaining 58 (61: 64: 67) sts.
1st row: p2, p2 tog, p to end of row.
2nd row: k to last 4 sts, k2 tog, k2.
Repeat these last 2 rows until 49 (52: 55: 58) sts remain. Continue straight for 26 rows and until work corresponds to back length. Leave sts on a s.st.h (for shoulder seam).

RIGHT FRONT
Work the same as left front reversing all shapings and *pocket position*. Work neck dec rows as follows:
1st row: p to last 4 sts, p2 tog tbl, p2.
2nd row: k2, sl.1, k1, psso, k to end of row.

Shoulder seam
Work 2 the same. With 3¼ mm (10) needles put 49 (52: 55: 58) sts from the back and the same from the front on to spare needles. Place these 2 needles side by side with the wrong sides of work facing each other. Then working on the right side of work, k tog a st from each needle to give 1 st on right hand needle. *K tog the next 2 sts (now 2 sts on right hand needle) then pass the 1st of these 2 sts over the 2nd. Repeat from * to work the rest of the sts.

FRONT BORDERS
Right side
With 2¾ mm (12) needles pick up the 11 sts

from s.st.h and work in k1, p1 twisted rib working a k st at all edges. Continue until border measures 4 cm (1½ in) less than front edge. Leave the 11 sts on a s.st.h. Mark the button positions, the 1st 1 cm (½ in), the 2nd 9 cm (3½ in) from cast on edge and 5 more evenly spaced allowing for 8th button in neck edge.

Left side
Work the same as right side working buttonholes to correspond to button positions.

Neck edge (version with round neck)
With right side facing and 2¾ mm (12) needles, start at right front border and rib 11 sts from s.st.h, k across 7 (8: 9: 10) sts on s.st.h, pick up and k 32 sts up side front, 1 st at shoulder seam, 3 sts down side back, 42 (44: 46: 48) sts on s.st.h (back neck edge), 3 sts up side back, 1 st at shoulder seam, 31 sts down side front, 7 (8: 9: 10) sts on s.st.h and rib 11 sts from left front border. (149: 153: 157: 161) sts. Work 9 rows in k1, p1 twisted rib working a buttonhole on the 4th row. Cast off loosely in rib.

Version with collar
With right side facing and 2¾ mm (12) needles, start at right front border, and rib 11 sts from s.st.h, k across 7 (8: 9: 10) sts on s.st.h, pick up and k 32 sts up side front, 1 st at shoulder seam, 42 (44: 46: 48) sts on s.st.h (back neck edge), 1 st at shoulder seam, 31 sts down side front, 7 (8: 9: 10) sts on s.st.h and rib 11 sts of left front border. (143: 147: 151: 155) sts. Work 8 rows in k1, p1 twisted rib working a buttonhole on the 4th row. Change to 3¼ mm (10) needles and work collar in k1, p1 twisted rib as follows:
1st row: k1, *k1, p1; repeat from * to last 2 sts, k2.
2nd row: (k1, p1) twice, inc into next st, rib to last 6 sts, inc into next st, rib to end of row.
3rd row: k2, p1, k1, p2, rib to last 6 sts, p2, k1, p1, k2.
4th row: as 2nd row.
Continue repeating these 4 rows until collar measures 7 cm (3 in) from beginning of 4 row repeat. Work 2 more rows without inc. Cast off loosely in rib.

Pocket tops
Work 2 the same. With 2¾ mm (12) needles pick up and k the 36 sts on s.st.h. Work 9 rows in k1, p1 twisted rib. Cast off loosely in rib.

SLEEVES

Work 2 the same. With right side facing and 3¼ mm (10) needles pick up and knit 9 sts on s.st.h (armhole shaping), 129 (137: 145: 153) sts evenly along armhole edge with centre stitch at shoulder seam and 9 sts on s.st.h. (147: 155: 163: 171) sts. Dec 1 st at each end of the 4th and every following 5th row as follows:

on k rows: k2, sl.1, k1, psso, k to last 4 sts, k2 tog, k2.

on p rows: p2, p2 tog, p to last 4 sts, p2 tog tbl, p2

until 83 (89: 95: 103) sts remain and work measures 46 (47: 48: 48) cm, 18 (18½: 19: 19) in.

Shape cuff

With wrong side facing
next row: dec 20 (22: 24: 28) sts evenly along row. (63: 67: 71: 75) sts.
Change to 2¾ mm (12) needles and work 10 cm (4 in) in k1, p1 twisted rib. Cast off loosely in rib.

MAKING UP

Work in all ends. Sew borders to fronts working the ease in equally, buttons to button band as marked, pocket linings to inside of fronts, pocket top edges to fronts, side and sleeve seams.

GEORGE
Man's slip-over in 4 ply wool

A traditional slip-over which can also be knitted in the smaller sizes for women with its roots deep in the heritage of Aran diamonds and furrows. Sweat shirt style detailing up-dates the traditional, cannily combining the old with the new. The front and back are patterned on a reverse stocking stitch base.

MATERIALS
6 (6: 7: 7: 8) 50 gm balls 4 ply wool
2 2¾ mm (12) needles
2 3¼ mm (10) needles
4 2¾ mm (12) double pointed needles or circular needle
cable needle
stitch holders

MEASUREMENTS
Chest
92 (97: 102: 107: 112) cm
36 (38: 40: 42: 44) in
Actual measurement
104 (109: 114: 119: 124) cm
41 (43: 45: 47: 49) in
Finished length to shoulder
66: (67: 68: 69: 70) cm
26 (26½: 27: 27½: 28) in

TENSION
30 sts and 36 rows for a 10 cm (4in) square worked in pattern on 3¼ mm (10) needles

BACK
*With 2¾ (12) needles cast on 124 (130: 138: 146: 154) sts and work 8 cms (3 ins) in k2, p2 rib. Change to 3¼ mm (10) needles and work next row as follows:
p 3 (2: 6: 10: 14) sts, *p3, inc into next st; repeat from * to last 5 (4: 8: 12: 16) sts, p to end of row. (153: 161: 169: 177: 185) sts. Work 1 row k.
Now work in pattern as follows with right side facing (r.st.st).
1st row: p 23 (27: 31: 35: 39) sts, *k1, p10, k2, p10, k1*, (p4, k1) 11 times, p4, repeat from * to *, p to end of row.

2nd row: k 23 (27: 31: 35: 39) sts, *p1, k10, p2, k10, p1*, (k4, p1) 11 times, k4, repeat from * to *, k to end of row.
3rd row: p 23 (27: 31: 35: 39) sts, *k1, p9, s1.1B, k1, pss, sl.1F, pl, kss, p9, k1* (p4, k1) 11 times, p4, repeat from * to *, p to end of row.
4th row: k 23(27: 31: 35: 39) sts, *p1, k9, p1, k2, p1, k9, p1*, (k4, p1) 11 times, k4, repeat from * to *, k to end of row.
5th row: p 23 (27: 31: 35: 39) sts, *k1, p8, s1.1B, k1, pss, p2, s1.1F, pl, kss, p8, k1 *, (p4, k1) 11 times, p4, repeat from * to *, p to end of row.
6th row: k 23 (27: 31: 35: 39) sts, *p1, k8, p1, k4, p1, k8, p1*, (k4, p1) 11 times, k4, repeat from * to *, k to end of row.
These last 4 rows set the pattern, continue as set, inc the diamonds by 2 sts every alternate row until the 20th row has been worked.
21st row: p 23 (27: 31: 35: 39) sts, *k1, p1, s1.1F, p1, kss, p16, s1.1B, k1, pss, p1, k1*, (p4, k1) 11 times, p4, repeat from * to *, p to end of row.
22nd row: k 23 (27: 31: 35: 39) sts, *p1, k2, p1, k16, p1, k2, p1*, (k4, p1) 11 times, k4, repeat from * to *, k to end of row.
23rd row: p 23 (27: 31: 35: 39) sts, *k1, p2, s1.1F, p1, kss, p14, s1.1B, k1, pss, p2, k1*, (p4, k1) 11 times, p4, repeat from * to *, p to end of row.
24th row: k 23 (27: 31: 35: 39) sts, *p1, k3, p1, k14, p1, k3, p1*, (k4, p1) 11 times, k4, repeat from * to *, k to end of row.
These last 4 rows set the pattern. Continue as set dec the diamonds by 2 sts every alternate row until the 37th row has been worked.

These last 36 rows set the pattern. Continue working 2nd to 37th rows inclusive until work measures 36 cm (14 in) from cast on edge.

Shape armhole

With right side facing k 7 sts and leave sts on a s.st.h, work to last 7 sts, put these on a s.st.h, turn, and continue on remaining 139 (147: 155: 163: 171) sts. Work 1 row. Keeping continuity

sts on a s.st.h for shoulder seam. Leave next 41 sts on a s.st.h for back neck edge. Rejoin wool to remaining 39 (43: 47: 51: 55) sts and work to end of row. Work to match other side reversing shaping and pattern.

FRONT

Work as for Back from * to *. Work straight for

of pattern correct now dec 1 st at each end of this and every alternate row until 119 (127: 135: 143: 151) sts remain.* Continue straight for 71 (75: 79: 83: 87) rows.

Shape neck

With right side facing work 39 (43: 47: 51: 55) sts, turn, and continue on these sts dec 1 st at neck edge on every row until 31 (35: 39: 43: 47) sts remain. Work 7 rows on these sts. Leave

10 (14: 20: 24: 28) rows.

Divide for front neck inset

With right side facing work 59 (63: 67: 71: 75) sts, turn, and continue on these sts dec 1 st at inset edge every alternate row until 39 (43: 47: 51: 55) sts remain. *Mark this row at neck edge on both sides*.

Shape neck

With right side facing dec 1 st at neck edge on

every row until 31 (35: 39: 43: 47) sts remain. Continue straight for 24 rows or until front corresponds to back length. Leave sts on a s.st.h for shoulder seam, putting the centre st of front on a separate s.st.h for front neck inset. Rejoin wool and work remaining 59 (63: 67: 71: 75) sts to match other side reversing shaping and pattern.

Shoulder seam

Work 2 the same. With 3¼ mm (10) needles put 31 (35: 39: 43: 47) sts from the back and the same from the front on to spare needles. Place these 2 needles side by side with wrong sides of work facing each other. Then working on the right side of work, k tog 1 st from each needle to give 1 st on right hand needle. *k tog the next 2 sts (now 2 sts on right hand needle) then pass the 1st of these 2 sts over the 2nd. Repeat from * to work the rest of the sts.

Front neck inset

With right side facing and 2¾ mm (12) needles pick up the centre front st on s.st.h and work p1, k1, p1 all into this stitch.

next row: inc into 1st st, p1, inc into last st.

next row: k1, p1 to last st, k1.

next row: inc into 1st st, k1, p1, k1, inc into last st.

Now continue in rib as set inc 1 st at each end

of every alternate row until there are 41 sts. Work 2 rows more without increasing. Leave sts on a s.st.h for front neck edge.

Neck edge

With right side facing and 4 2¾ mm (12) double pointed needles or circular needle and starting at side front at neck shaping mark, pick up and k 26 sts up side front, 1 st at shoulder seam, 12 sts down side back, 41 sts from s.st.h (back neck edge), 12 sts up side back, 1 st at shoulder seam, 26 sts down side front and rib across 41 sts of front neck inset. (160) sts. Work 9 rounds in k1, p1 rib. Cast off *loosely* in rib. *Make sure a man can get his head through.*

Armhole edges

Work 2 the same. With right side facing and 4 2¾ mm (12) double pointed needles or circular needle pick up and k 7 sts from s.st.h, 158 (166: 174: 182: 190) sts evenly around armhole edge with centre st at shoulder seam and 7 sts from s.st.h (172: 180: 188: 196: 204) sts. Divide evenly on to 3 needles and work 9 rounds in k1, p1 rib. Cast off loosely in rib so that edge is neither frilly or tight.

MAKING UP

Work in all ends, sew V inset neatly into front and sew side seams.

HOCKEY
Ladies jumper in double knit wool

The sweat shirt shape taken to great lengths: all the advantages of a casual sporty garment and warm, flattering length. The fully fashioned body is in stocking stitch, the cuffs and welts are in 2x2 rib and the sweat shirt neckline is in 1x1 rib. Take special care when sewing in the V inset.

MATERIALS
11 (12: 12: 13) 50 gm balls double knit wool
2 3¼ mm (10) needles
2 4 mm (8) needles
4 3¼ mm (10) double pointed needles
stitch holders

MEASUREMENTS
Bust
86 (91: 97: 102) cm
34 (36: 38: 40) in
Measurement at widest point
99 (104: 109: 114) cm
39 (41: 43: 45) in
Finished length to shoulder
70 (71: 72: 73) cm
27½ (28: 28 ½: 29) in
Sleeve length
52 (53: 54: 54) cm
20½ (21: 21½: 21½) in

TENSION
22 sts and 30 rows for a 10 cm (4 in) square worked in st.st on 4 mm (8) needles

BACK
* With 3¼ mm (10) needles cast on 106 (112: 118: 124) sts. Work 9 cm (3½ in) in k2, p2 twisted rib (k into back of k sts). Change to 4 mm (8) needles and continue in st.st inc 1 st at the end of the 1st row. (107: 113: 119: 125) sts. Continue straight on these sts until work measures 47 cm (18½ in) from cast on edge.
Shape armholes
With right side facing k 8 sts and put these sts on a s.st.h, work to last 8 sts and put these sts on a s.st.h. Turn and continue on remaining 91

(97: 103: 109) sts.* Continue straight for 57 (61: 65: 69) rows.
Shape neck
With right side facing
next row: k 30 (33: 36: 39) sts, turn and continue on these sts.
1st row: p2, p2 tog, p to end of row.
2nd row: k to last 4 sts, k2 tog, k2.
Repeat these last 2 rows until 23 (26: 29: 32) sts remain. Work 4 rows. Leave sts on a s.st.h for shoulder seam, leave next 31 sts on a s.st.h for back neck edge. Rejoin yarn and continue on remaining 30 (33: 36: 39) sts, k to end of row. Work to match other side reversing shaping and working dec rows as follows:
1st row: p to last 4 sts, p2 tog tbl, p2.
2nd row: k2, sl.1, k1, psso, k to end of row.

FRONT
Work the same as Back from * to *. Continue straight for 11 (15: 19: 23) rows.
Divide for front neck inset
With right side facing k 45 (48: 51: 54) sts, turn and continue on these sts dec 1 st at inset edge every alternate row (*not fully fashioned*) until 30 (33: 36: 39) sts remain. *Mark this row at neck edge on both sides.*
Shape neck
With right side facing (*fully fashioned*)
1st row: k to last 4 sts, k2 tog, k2.
2nd row: p2, p2 tog, p to end of row.
Repeat these last 2 rows until 23 (26: 29: 32) sts remain. Continue straight until work corresponds to back length (19 rows). Leave sts on s.st.h for shoulder seam, leave centre st of front on a s.st.h for front neck inset. Rejoin yarn and work remaining 45 (48: 51: 54) sts to

match other side reversing shapings and working *neck shaping* dec as follows:

1st row: k2, sl.1, k1, psso, k to end of row.
2nd row: p to last 4 sts, p2 tog tbl, p2.

Shoulder seam

Work 2 the same. With 4 mm (8) needles put 23 (26: 29: 32) sts from the back and the same from the front on to spare needles. Place these 2 needles side by side with the wrong sides of work facing each other. Then working on right side of work k tog a st from each needle to give 1 st on right hand needle. *K tog the next 2 sts, (now 2 sts on right hand needle) then pass the 1st of these 2 sts over the 2nd. Repeat from * to work the rest of the sts.

Front neck inset

With right side facing work in k1, p1 twisted rib. With 3¼ mm (10) needles pick up the st on the s.st.h and work p1, k1, p1 all into this stitch.
next row: inc into 1st st, p1, inc into last st.
next row: k1, p1, to last st, k1.
next row: inc into 1st st, k1, p1, k1, inc into last st.
Now continue in rib as set inc 1 st at each end of every alternate row until there are 31 sts. Work 2 more rows in rib without inc. Leave sts on a s.st.h for front neck edge.

Neck edge

With right side facing and 4 3¼ mm (10) double pointed needles, start at side front. Pick up and k 22 sts up side front, 1 st at shoulder seam, 10 sts down side back, 31 sts from s.st.h (back neck edge), 10 sts up side back, 1 st at shoulder seam, 22 sts down side front and rib across 31 sts of front neck inset. (128 sts) Work 7 rounds in k1, p1 rib (every other row twisted). Cast off in rib. *Make sure you can get your head through.*

SLEEVES

Work 2 the same. With right side facing and 4 mm (8) needles, pick up and k 8 sts from s.st.h (armhole shaping), 99 (105: 111: 117) sts evenly along armhole edge with centre stitch at shoulder seam and 8 sts from s.st.h. (115: 121: 127: 133) sts. Now dec 1 st at each end of the 2nd and every following 4th row as follows: k2, s1.1, k1, psso, k to last 4 sts, k2 tog, k2 until 51 (55: 59: 65) sts remain.

Shape cuff

With wrong side facing
next row: dec 9 (11: 13: 17) sts evenly along the row. (42: 44: 46: 48) sts.
Change to 3¼ mm (10) needles and work 9 cm (3½ in) in k2, p2 twisted rib. Cast off loosely in rib.

MAKING UP

Work in all ends. Sew V inset neatly into front, sew side and sleeve seams.

LLOYD
Pullover for men in double knit wool

A rugged sensible jumper with the stamp of the country all over it — deep furrows of wide ribs and panels of moss stitch centred with an important cable. It can be knitted with either a rolled round neck or a fully fashioned ribbed collar.

MATERIALS
15 (15: 16: 16) 50 gm balls double knit wool
2 3¼ mm (10) needles
2 4 mm (8) needles
4 3¼ mm (10) double pointed needles
4 4 mm (8) double pointed needles
1 cable needle
stitch holders

MEASUREMENTS
Chest
97 (102: 107: 112) cm
38 (40 :42: 44) in
Approx actual measurement
111 (116: 121: 124) cm
43½ (45½: 47½: 49) in
Finished length to shoulder
67 (69: 70: 71) cm
26½ (27: 27½: 28) in
Sleeve length
55 (56: 58: 58) cm
21½ (22: 23: 23) in

TENSION
25 sts and 30 rows for a 10 cm (4 in) square worked in pattern on 4 mm (8) needles

BACK
*With 3¼ mm (10) needles, cast on 102 (108: 114: 120) sts. Work 8 cm (3 in) in k2, p2 rib. Change to 4 mm (8) needles and work next row in k inc 34 sts evenly across row. (136: 142: 148: 154) sts.
next row: p.
Now continue in pattern as follows:
1st row: before pattern: k0 (k2, p1: p1, k4, p1: k2, p2, k4, p1), pattern: p1 (k4, p2) 5 times, k4, p4, work 11 sts in moss st, p4, k4, p4, k12, p4,
k4, p4, work 11 sts in moss st, p4, k4 (p2, k4) 5 times, p1, after pattern: k0 (p1, k2: p1, k4, p1: p1,k4, p2, k2).
2nd row: before pattern: p0 (3: 6: 9) sts, pattern: p35, k4, work 11 sts in moss st, k4, p4, k4, p12, k4, p4, k4, work 11 sts in moss st, k4, p35, after pattern: p0 (3: 6: 9) sts.
Repeat these last 2 rows 10 more times (all sizes).
23rd row: work the sts as set before pattern then
p1, (k4, p2) 5 times, k4, p4, work 11 sts in moss st, p4, k4, p4, cable next 12 sts thus, slip the first 6 sts on to a cable needle and leave at front of work, k6, k6 sts from cable needle, p4, k4, p4, work 11 sts in moss st, p4, k4, (p2, k4) 5 times, p1,
then work sts as set after pattern to end of row.
24th row: work 2nd row.
These last 24 rows make one pattern. Repeat throughout keeping continuity correct over dec. When work measures 42 cm (16½ in) from cast on edge,
Shape armholes
With right side facing work the first 5 sts and put these sts on a s.st.h, work to the last 5 sts and put them on a s.st.h, turn and continue on remaining 126 (132: 138: 144) sts. * Work straight for 72 (76: 80: 84) rows. Leave all sts on a s.st.h for shoulders and back neck edge.

FRONT
Work the same as Back from * to *. Work straight for 44 (48: 52: 56) rows.
Shape neck
With right side facing work 53 (55: 57: 59) sts, turn and continue on these sts dec 1 st at neck edge on next and every following row until 42

(44: 46: 48) sts remain. Continue straight until front corresponds to back length (16 rows). Leave sts on a s.st.h for shoulder seam. Leave centre 20 (22: 24: 26) sts on a s.st.h (front neck edge) and continue on remaining 53 (55: 57: 59) sts. Rejoin wool, work to end of row and

(now 2 sts on right hand needle) then pass the 1st of these 2 sts over the 2nd. Repeat from * to work rest of sts.

VERSION WITH COLLAR
With right side facing and 4 3¼ mm (10)

work to match other side of front reversing shaping.

Shoulder seam

Work 2 the same. With 4 mm (8) needles put 42 (44: 46: 48) sts from the back and the same from the front on to spare needles. Place these 2 needles side by side with the wrong sides of work facing each other. Then working on right side of work k tog a st from each needle to give 1 st on right hand needle. *K tog the next 2 sts

double pointed needles start at centre front. Pick up and k 10 (11: 12: 13) sts from s.st.h (half of front neck edge), 23 sts up side front, 1 st from shoulder seam, 42 (44: 46: 48) sts from s.st.h (back neck edge), 1 st from shoulder seam, 22 sts down side front and remaining 10 (11: 12: 13) sts from s.st.h. (109: 113: 117: 121 sts). Work 8 rounds in k1, p1 rib with the 2 centre front sts as k sts. Now divide for collar. Change to 4 4 mm (8) double pointed needles and work in rows. At centre front, turn.

1st row: k1, *k1, p1; repeat from * to last 2 sts, k2.

2nd row: (k1, p1) twice, inc into next st, rib to last 6 sts, inc into next st, rib to end of row.

3rd row: k2, p1, k1, p2, rib to last 6 sts, p2, k1, p1, k2.

4th row: work as 2nd row.

Continue repeating these 4 rows until collar measures 10 cm (4 in) from pick up row. Work two more rows without inc. Cast off loosely in rib.

VERSION WITH ROLLED NECK EDGE

With right side facing and 4 3¼ mm (10) double pointed needles pick up and k 1 st at shoulder seam, 42 (44: 46: 48) sts on s.st.h (back neck edge), 1 st at shoulder seam, 22 sts down side front, 20 (22: 24: 26) sts on s.st.h (front neck edge) and 22 sts up side front. (108: 112: 116: 120 sts) Work 20 rounds in k1, p1 rib. Cast off loosely in rib. *Make sure a man can get his head through.*

SLEEVES

Work 2 the same. With right side facing and 4 mm (8) needles, pick up and k 5 sts on s.st.h (armhole shaping), 116 (122: 128: 134) sts evenly along armhole edge with centre at shoulder seam and 5 sts from s.st.h. (126: 132: 138: 144 sts) Work 1 row p. Now work in pattern as follows at the same time dec 1 st at each end of the 3rd and every following 4th row.

1st row: before pattern: k0 (p1, k2: k2, p2, k2: p1, k4, p2, k2) pattern: k2, (p2, k4) 20 times, p2, k2, after pattern: k0 (k2, p1: k2, p2, k2: k2, p2, k4, p1).

2nd row: p.

These 2 rows set the pattern. Continue repeating throughout sleeve keeping continuity correct over dec until 56 (60: 64: 70) sts remain.

Shape cuff

With wrong side facing dec 8 (10: 12: 16) sts evenly across row to leave 48 (50: 52: 54) sts. Change to 3¼ mm (10) needles and work 8 cm (3 in) in k2, p2 rib. Cast off loosely in rib.

MAKING UP

Work in all ends, sew side and sleeve seams. Sew down rolled neck edge to inside so that neck edge will still give sufficiently to pull over head, work a strengthening stitch on the inside of centre front where collar divides.

DAISY

Girl's sweater in 4 ply wool, for 4 to 10 years

A traditional smock shape which can be dressed up or down to be either sporty or pretty. It is boxy and crisp with two neat little pockets and a collar. For greater emphasis these are worked in garter stitch to contrast with the stocking stitch used for the body of the sweater.

MATERIALS
6 (7: 7: 8) 50 gm balls 4 ply wool
2 2¾ mm (12) needles
2 3¼ mm (10) needles
4 2¾ mm (12) double pointed needles
stitch holders

MEASUREMENTS
66 (71: 76: 81) cm
26 (28: 30: 32) in
Measurement at widest point
79 (84: 89: 94) cm
31 (33: 35: 37) in
Finished length to shoulder
41 (44: 48: 52) cm
16 (17½: 19: 20½) in
Sleeve length
37 (41: 44: 48) cm
14½ (16: 17½: 19) in

TENSION
28 sts and 36 rows for a 10 cm (4 in) square worked in st.st on 3¼ mm (10) needles

BACK
With 2¾ mm (12) needles cast on 108 (116: 124: 132) sts. Work 20 rows in g.st. Change to 3¼ mm (10) needles and continue in st.st. Work straight until work measures 25 (28: 31: 33) cm (10: 11: 12: 13) in from cast on edge.
Shape armholes
With right side facing k the first 7 sts and put them on a s.st.h, work to the last 7 sts and put these on a s.st.h, turn and continue on remaining 94 (102: 110: 118) sts. Work straight for 55 (59: 63: 67) rows. Leave all sts on a s.st.h for shoulder seams and collar.

Pocket linings
Work 2 the same. With 3¼ mm (10) needles, cast on 26 sts and work 28 rows in st.st. Leave sts on a s.st.h.

FRONT
Work the same as Back but place 2 pockets as follows:
work as Back until 28 rows have been worked in st.st.
next row: with right side facing k 9 sts, slip next 26 sts on to a s.st.h, and in place of these k across 26 sts of pocket lining, k 38 (46: 54: 62) sts, slip next 26 sts on to a s.st.h and in place of these k across 26 sts of other pocket lining, k remaining 9 sts. Now continue as given for Back.
Shoulder seam
Work 2 the same. With 3¼ mm (10) needles put 22 (25: 28: 31) sts from the Back and the same from the Front on to spare needles. Place these 2 needles side by side with the wrong sides of work facing each other. Then working on the right side of work k tog a st from each needle to give 1 st on right hand needle. *K tog the next 2 sts (now 2 sts on right hand needle) then pass the 1st of these 2 sts over the 2nd. Repeat from * to work the rest of the sts.
Pocket tops
Work 2 the same. With right side facing and 2¾ mm (12) needles, pick up and k 26 sts on s.st.h. Work 8 rows in g.st. Cast off loosely on wrong side of work.

SLEEVES
Work 2 the same. With right side facing and 3¼ mm (10) needles, pick up and k 7 sts from

s.st.h (armhole shaping), 83 (91: 99: 107) sts along armhole edge with centre st at shoulder seam and 7 sts from s.st.h. (97: 105: 113: 121) sts. Now dec 1 st at each end of every 5th row as follows:

on k rows: k2, sl.1, k1, psso, k to last 4 sts, k2 tog, k2.

on p rows: p2, p2 tog, p to last 4 sts, p2 tog tbl, p2

until 55 (57: 59: 61) sts remain and work measures 30 (34: 38: 42) cm 12 (13½: 15: 16½) in.

Shape cuff
With wrong side facing dec 17 (15: 13: 11) sts evenly across row. (38: 42: 46: 50) sts. Change to 2¾ mm (12) needles and work 6 cm (2½ in) in k2, p2 rib. Cast off loosely in rib.

COLLAR
With right side facing and 4 2¾ mm (12) double pointed needles, start at centre front. Pick up and k 25 (26: 27: 28) sts from s.st.h (half of front neck edge), 1 st from shoulder seam, 50 (52: 54: 56) sts from s.st.h (back neck edge), 1 st from shoulder seam and 25 (26: 27: 28) sts from s.st.h. (102: 106: 110: 114) sts. Work 10 rounds in k1, p1 rib. Now work collar. Starting at centre front, turn and work in g.st in rows on these sts until collar measures 5 cm (2 in). Cast off on underside of collar (do not pull in or flute).

MAKING UP
Work in all ends. Sew pocket linings to inside of front, pocket top edges to front and side and sleeve seams. Sew a neat strengthening stitch on inside of neck edge where collar divides.

LILLIAN
Ladies beaded cardigan in 4 ply wool

An elegant little cardigan knitted in stocking stitch but with beads knitted in to the work to give the look of 'polka dots'. There are instructions on how to thread the beads on to the wool. This cardigan can be worn over the jumper Dorothy.

MATERIALS
10 (10: 11: 11) 50 gm balls 4 ply wool
2 2¾ mm (12) needles
2 3¼ mm (10) needles
stitch holders
10 buttons 1.5 cm (½ in) diameter
approximately 600 (600: 700: 700) beads (hole in bead must be big enough to pass through wool on a fine darning needle)

MEASUREMENTS
Bust
86 (91: 97: 102) cm
34 (36: 38: 40) in
Actual measurement
99 (104: 109: 114) cm
39 (41: 43: 45) in
Finished length to shoulder
60 (61: 62: 63) cm
23½ (24: 24½: 25) in
Sleeve length
55 (56: 57: 57) cm
21½ (22: 22½: 22½) in

TENSION
28 sts and 36 rows for a 10 cm (4 in) square worked in st.st on 3¼ mm (10) needles

BACK
With 2¾ mm (12) needles cast on 117 (125: 133: 141) sts. Work 11 cm (4½ in) in kl, pl twisted rib (k into back of k sts). Change to 3¼ mm (10) needles. Before starting to work pattern, thread approx 80 beads per ball on to yarn (using fine darning needle, thread yarn on to needle and pass through hole of beads). Continue in pattern as follows and *at the same time* inc 1 st at each end of 9th and every

following 10th row.
1st row: with right side facing k2 (6: 3: 0) sts, *k7, k1 with bead, k6; repeat from * to last 3 (7: 4: 1) sts, k to end of row.
Work 9 rows in st.st working inc as set.
11th row: k3 (7: 4: 1) sts, *k1 with bead, k13, repeat from * to last 4 (8: 5: 2) sts, k1 with bead, k to end of row.
Work 9 rows in st.st working inc as set. These last 20 rows make one pattern. Continue as set keeping continuity correct over incs and pattern until there are 137 (145: 153: 161) sts. Work 4 more rows. Work should measure approx 41 cm (16 in) from cast on edge.

Shape armholes
With right side facing work 7 sts at beginning of next 2 rows, and put these sts on s.st.h (123: 131: 139: 147) sts. Continue straight for 62 (66: 70: 74) rows.

Shape neck
With right side facing k 39 (42: 45: 48) sts, turn and continue on these sts. Work 3 rows then leave sts on a s.st.h for shoulder seam. Leave next 45 (47: 49: 51) sts on a s.st.h for back neck edge. Rejoin yarn and work remaining 39 (42: 45: 48) sts and work to match other side.

Pocket lining for left front
With 3¼ mm (10) needles cast on 20 sts and work 7½ cm (3 in) in st.st. Leave sts on s.st.h.

LEFT FRONT
With 2¾ mm (12) needles cast on 65 (69: 73: 77) sts. Work in k1, p1 twisted rib, working a k st at all edges and starting 1st row thus: k2, *p1, k1; repeat from * to last st, k1. Continue in pattern until rib measures 11 cm (4½ in). Change to 3¼ mm (10) needles and work in pattern as given for back and *at the*

same time inc 1 st at side edge on 9th and every 10th row starting as follows:

1st row: with right side facing k 2 (6: 3: 0) sts, *k7, k1 with bead, k6; repeat from * to last 21 (21: 14: 21) sts. On these sts for *1st, 2nd* and *4th* sizes work as follows: k7, k1 with bead, k2, leave remaining 11 sts on a s.st.h for front border.

For *3rd* size work k3 and leave remaining 11 sts on a s.st.h for front border.

Turn and continue on remaining 54 (58: 62: 66) sts. This sets the position of the pattern. Continue as set keeping continuity correct over incs and pattern until there are 64 (68: 72: 76) sts. Work a further 4 rows when front should correspond to back length.

Shape armholes
With right side facing k 7 sts and put these sts on a s.st.h, k to end of row. (57: 61: 65: 69) sts. Work 1 row.

Place pocket lining
With right side facing and working from armhole edge k 13 (17: 21: 25) sts, slip next 20 sts on to a s.st.h and in place of these k across the 20 sts of pocket lining, k to end of row. Continue straight for a further 29 (33: 37: 41) rows.

Shape neck
With right side facing work to last 8 (9: 10: 11) sts and put these sts on a s.st.h for front neck edge. Turn and continue on remaining 49 (52: 55: 58) sts and work to end of row. Dec 1 st at neck edge every row until 39 (42: 45: 48) sts remain. Continue straight for 25 rows when front should correspond to back length. Leave sts on a s.st.h.

To make a buttonhole
With right side facing k2, (p1, k1) twice, yarn round needle, k2 tog, work to end of row.

RIGHT FRONT
Work as for left front but reversing all shapings and patterning and *omitting the pocket* as well as working 3 buttonholes into the ribbing, the 1st 1 cm (½ in), the 2nd 6 cm (2½ in) from cast on edge and the 3rd on the last but one row of ribbing. Continue in pattern as follows:

1st, 2nd and *4th* sizes: put the 1st 11 sts on a s.st.h for front border, k2, k1 with bead, k7, *k6, k1 with bead, k7; repeat from * to last 2 (6: 0) sts, k to end of row.

3rd size: put the 1st 11 sts on a s.st.h for front border, k3, *k6, k1 with bead, k7; repeat from * to last 3 sts, k to end of row. This sets the position of the pattern.

FRONT BORDERS
Left side
With 2¾ mm (12) needles pick up the 11 sts on s.st.h and work in k1, p1 twisted rib working a k st at all edges. Work until border measures 4 cm (1½ in) less than front edge. Leave the 11 sts on a s.st.h. Mark the button positions, the 1st 1 cm (½ in), the 2nd 6 cm (2½ in), the 3rd 11 cm (4½ in) from cast on edge and 6 more evenly spaced allowing for a 10th button in the neck edge.

Right side
Work the same as left side working buttonholes to correspond to button positions. Leave the 11 sts on a s.st.h.

Shoulder seam
Work 2 the same. With 3¼ mm (10) needles put 39 (42: 45: 48) sts from the back and the same from the front on to spare needles. Place these 2 needles side by side with the wrong sides of work facing each other. Then working on the right side of work, k tog a st from each needle to give 1 st on right hand needle. *K tog the next 2 sts (now 2 sts on right hand needle) then pass the 1st of these 2 sts over the 2nd. Repeat from * to work the rest of the sts.

Neck edge
With right side facing and 2¾ mm (12) needles, start at right front border. Rib 11 sts from s.st.h (border), k across 8 (9: 10: 11) sts on s.st.h, pick up and k 32 sts up side front, 1 st from shoulder seam, 3 sts down side back, 45 (47: 49: 51) sts on s.st.h (back neck edge), 3 sts up side back, 1 st from shoulder seam, 32 sts down side front, 8 (9: 10: 11) sts on s.st.h and rib across 11 sts of left front border. (155: 159: 163: 167) sts. Work 9 rows in k1, p1 twisted rib working a buttonhole on the 4th row. Cast off loosely in rib.

Pocket top
With 2¾ mm (12) needles pick up and k the 20 sts on s.st.h then work 9 rows in k1, p1 twisted rib. Cast off loosely in rib.

SLEEVES
Work 2 the same. With right side facing and

3¼ mm (10) needles pick up and k 7 sts on s.st.h (armhole shaping), 103 (111: 119: 127) sts evenly along armhole edge with centre stitch at shoulder seam and 7 sts on s.st.h. (117: 125: 133: 141) sts. Work 3 rows in st.st. Now work in pattern as given for back starting as follows and *at the same time* dec 1 st at each end of the next and every following 5th row.
1st row: (dec row with right side facing) k2 tog, k0 (4: 1: 5) sts, *k7, k1 with bead, k6; repeat from * to last 3 (7: 4: 8) sts, k1 (5: 2: 6), k2 tog. (115: 123: 131: 139) sts. This sets the position of the pattern. Continue as set keeping continuity correct over decs and pattern until 57 (63: 69: 77) sts remain and sleeve measures 44 (45: 46: 46) cm 17 (17½: 18: 18) in. Change to 2¾ mm (12) needles and work 11 cm (4½ in) in k1, p1 twisted rib. Cast off loosely in rib.

MAKING UP
Work in all ends, sew borders to fronts working ease in evenly, sew side and sleeve seams, pocket top edges to front, pocket lining to inside of front and buttons to button positions.

DOROTHY
Ladies beaded jumper in 4 ply wool

A perfect partner for the cardigan Lillian with its matching
beading, this jumper is short, waisted and very feminine with
the fully fashioned collar in a neat rib.

MATERIALS
8 (9: 9: 10) 50 gm balls 4 ply wool
2 2¾ mm (12) needles
2 3¼ mm (10) needles
4 2¾ mm (12) double pointed needles
4 3¼ mm (10) double pointed needles
stitch holders
approximately 600 (650: 650: 750) beads (hole
in bead must be big enough to pass through
wool on a fine darning needle)

MEASUREMENTS
Bust
86 (91: 97: 102) cm
34 (36: 38: 40) in
Actual measurement
94 (99: 104: 109) cm
37 (39: 41: 43) in
Finished length to shoulder
57 (58: 59: 60) cm
22½ (23: 23½: 24) in
Sleeve length
53 (54: 56: 56) cm
21 (21½: 22: 22) cm

TENSION
28 sts and 36 rows for a 10 cm (4 in) square
worked in st.st on 3¼ mm (10) needles

BACK
* With 2¾ mm (12) needles cast on 109 (117:
125: 133) sts. Work 11 cm (4½ in) in k1, p1
twisted rib (k into back of k sts). Change to 3¼
mm (10) needles. Before starting to knit pattern,
thread approx 80 beads per ball on to yarn
(using a fine darning needle, thread yarn on to
needle and pass through hole of beads).
Continue in pattern as follows and *at the same
time* inc 1 st at each end of 5th and every

following 10th row.
1st row: with right side facing k5 (2: 6: 3) sts,
*k7, k1 with bead, k6; repeat from * to last 6 (3:
7: 4) sts, k to end of row.
Work 9 rows in st.st working inc as set.
11th row: k6, (3: 7: 4) sts, *k1 with bead, k13;
repeat from * to last 7 (4: 8: 5) sts, k1 with
bead, k to end of row.
Work 9 rows in st.st working inc as set. These
last 20 rows make one pattern. Continue as set
keeping continuity correct over incs and
pattern until there are 129 (137: 145: 153) sts.
Work a further 6 rows. Work should measure
approx 39 cm (15½ in) from cast on edge.
Shape armholes
With right side facing work 7 sts at beginning of
next 2 rows, and put these sts on a s.st.h. (115:
123: 131: 139) sts.* Continue straight for 62
(66: 70: 74) rows. Leave all sts on s.st.h for
shoulder seams (36: 39: 42: 45) sts each and
back neck edge (43: 45: 47: 49) sts.

FRONT
Work the same as Back from * to *. Continue
straight for 30 (34: 38: 42) rows.
Shape neck
With right side facing
next row: k 46 (49: 52: 55) sts, turn, and
continue on these sts, dec 1 st every row at
neck edge until 36 (39: 42: 45) sts remain.
Continue straight for 21 rows when front should
correspond to back length. Leave sts on s.st.h
for shoulder seam. Leave next 23 (25: 27: 29)
sts on a s.st.h for front neck edge. Rejoin yarn
to remaining 46 (49: 52: 55) sts and work to
match other side.
Shoulder seam
Work 2 the same. With 3¼ mm needles put 36
(39: 42: 45) sts from the back and the same

from the front on to spare needles. Place these 2 needles side by side with the wrong sides of work facing each other. Then working on the right side of work, k tog a st from each needle to give 1 st on right hand needle. *K tog the next 2 sts (now 2 sts on right hand needle) then pass the 1st of these 2 sts over the 2nd. Repeat from * to work the rest of the sts.

SLEEVES

With right side facing work 2 the same. With 3¼ mm (10) needles pick up and k 7 sts on s.st.h (armhole shaping), 99 (107: 115: 123) sts evenly along armhole edge with centre stitch at shoulder seam and 7 sts on s.st.h. (113: 121: 129: 137) sts. Work 5 rows in st.st. Now work in pattern as given for Back starting as follows and *at the same time* dec 1 st at each end of the next and every following 6th row.

1st row: with right side facing (dec row) k2 tog, k5 (2: 6: 3) sts, *k7, k1 with bead, k6; repeat from * to last 8 (5: 9: 6) sts, k6 (3: 7: 4) sts, k2 tog. (111: 119: 127: 135) sts. This sets the position of the pattern. Continue as set keeping continuity correct over dec and pattern until 63 (71: 77: 85) sts remain.

Shape cuff

next row: dec 6 (8: 10: 16) sts evenly along row. (57: 63: 67: 69) sts. Change to 2¾ mm (12) needles and work 11 cm (4½ in) in k1, p1 twisted rib. Cast off loosely in rib.

Neck edge and collar

With right side facing and 4 2¾ mm (12) double pointed needles, start at centre front. Pick up and k 12 (13: 14: 15) sts from s.st.h (front neck edge), 28 sts up side front, 1 st at shoulder seam, 43 (45: 47: 49) sts from s.st.h (back neck edge), 1 st at shoulder seam, 27 sts down side front and remaining 11 (12: 13: 14) sts from s.st.h (front neck edge). (123: 127: 131: 135) sts. Work 7 rounds in k1, p1 rib with every alternate round in k1, p1 twisted rib keeping the two centre front sts as k sts. Now divide for collar. Change to 4 3¼ mm (10) double pointed needles, turn, and work in rows in k1, p1 twisted rib.

1st row: k1, *k1, p1; repeat from * to last st, k1.

2nd row: (k1, p1) twice, inc into next st, rib to last 6 sts, inc into next st, rib to end of row.

3rd row: k2, p1, k1, p2, rib to last 6 sts, p2, k1, p1, k2.

4th row: work as 2nd row.

Continue repeating these 4 rows until collar measures 5 cm (2 in) from beginning of 4 row repeat. Work 2 more rows without increasing. Cast off loosely in rib.

MAKING UP

Work in all ends, sew side and sleeve seams. Work a neat oversew strengthening stitch at the inside of centre front neck where the collar divides.

ROCKY
Man's slip-over in thick cotton

A traditional man's slip-over with all the undertones of a British summer. The body is worked in moss stitch with a centre panel of wide ribs and the two main cables are flanked with stocking stitch panels. The V neck and armholes are edged with a rolled rib.

MATERIALS
9 (9: 10: 10) 50 gm balls thick-weight cotton
2 3 mm (11) needles
2 3¾ mm (9) needles
4 3 mm (11) double pointed needles
cable needle
stitch holders

MEASUREMENTS
Chest
97 (102: 107: 112) cm
38 (40: 42: 44) in
Measurement at widest point
107 (112: 117: 122) cm
42 (44: 46: 48:) in
Finished length to shoulder
65 (66: 67: 68) cm
25½ (26: 26½: 27) in

TENSION
26 sts and 33 rows for a 10 cm (4 in) square worked in pattern on 3¾ mm (9) needles

BACK
* With 3 mm (11) needles cast 110 (116: 122: 128) sts. Work 9 cm (3½ in) in k2, p2 rib. Change to 3¾ mm (9) needles.
next row: k 7 (10: 13: 16) sts, *inc into next st, k3; repeat from * to last 3 (6: 9: 12) sts, k to end of row (135: 141: 147: 153) sts.
Now continue in pattern as follows:
1st row: with wrong side facing work 19 (22: 25: 28) sts in moss st ending with a k st, p4, k2, p6, k2, p4, work 13 sts in moss st thus: (k1, p1 to last st, k1), p 35, work 13 sts in moss st thus: (k1, p1 to last st, k1), p4, k2, p6, k2, p4, work in moss st to end of row.

2nd row: work 19 (22: 25: 28) sts in moss st, k4, p2, k6, p2, k4, work 13 sts in moss st thus: (k1, p1 to last st, k1), (k5, p1) 5 times, k5, work 13 sts in moss st thus: (k1, p1 to last st, k1), k4, p2, k6, p2, k4, work in moss st to end of row.
These 2 rows set the pattern of the rib. Work 5 more rows keeping continuity correct.
8th row: work 19 (22: 25: 28) sts in moss st, k4, p2, cable next 6 sts thus: put first 3 sts on a cable needle and leave at front of work, k3, k3 sts from cable needle, p2, k4, work 13 sts in moss st, (k5, p1) 5 times, k5, work 13 sts in moss st, k4, p2, cable next 6 sts, p2, k4, work in moss st to end of row.
These last 8 rows (1st to 8th) make the pattern. Continue repeating these rows throughout. Work straight until work measures 37 cm (14½ in) from cast on edge.
Shape armholes
With right side facing and keeping continuity of pattern correct, work the first 8 sts in moss st and put them on a s.st.h, work to last 8 sts and put these sts on a s.st.h. Turn and continue on remaining 119 (125: 131: 137) sts. Now dec 1 st at each end of every row until 105 (111: 117: 123) sts remain.* Work straight for 75 (79: 83: 87) rows.
Shape neck
With right side facing work 28 (31: 34: 37) sts, turn and work a further 3 rows on these sts. Leave on s.st.h for shoulder seam. Leave centre 49 sts on a s.st.h for back neck edge. Rejoin yarn and continue on remaining 28 (31: 34: 37) sts. Work to match other side.

FRONT
Work the same as Back from * to *.

Divide and shape for V neck

With right side facing work 52 (55: 58: 61) sts, turn and continue on these sts keeping pattern correct. Dec 1 st at neck edge on every 3rd row until 28 (31: 34: 37) sts remain. Work straight until work corresponds to back length. Leave sts on a s.st.h for shoulder seam. Leave centre st on a s.st.h for neck edge, rejoin yarn and continue on remaining 52 (55: 58: 61) sts. Work to match other side.

Shoulder seam

Work 2 the same. With 3¾ mm (9) needles put 28 (31: 34: 37) sts from the back and the same from the front on to spare needles. Place these 2 needles side by side with wrong sides of work facing each other. Then working on right side of work k tog a stitch from each needle to give 1 st on right hand needle. *K tog the next 2 sts (now 2 sts on right hand needle) then pass the 1st of these 2 sts over the 2nd. Repeat from * to work rest of stitches.

Neck edge

With right side facing and 4 3 mm (11) double pointed needles, start at shoulder. Pick up and k 1 st at shoulder seam, 3 sts down side back, 49 sts on s.st.h, 3 sts up side back, 1 st at shoulder seam, 69 sts down side front, 1 st from s.st.h (centre front) and 69 sts up side front. (196 sts) Now work 9 rounds in k1, p1 rib as follows: (the centre front st must be knit)

1st round: (k1, p1) for 124 sts, p2 tog tbl, k1, p2 tog, (p1, k1) to last st, p1.

2nd round: rib to 2 sts before centre st, p2 tog tbl, k1, p2 tog, rib to complete round.

When 9 dec rounds have been worked, work a further 9 rounds inc 1 st either side of centre st each round. Cast off loosely in rib.

Armhole edges

Work 2 the same. With right side facing and 4 3 mm (11) double pointed needles, pick up and k 8 sts from s.st.h (armhole shaping), 122 sts along armhole edge with centre at shoulder seam and 8 sts from s.st.h. (138 sts) Work 18 rounds in k1, p1 rib. Cast off in rib.

MAKING UP

Work in all ends. Sew side seams. Sew rolled neck and armhole edges to inside of work.

BOSANOVA
Ladies jumper in thick cotton

Double dramatic V-neck sweater, back and front a mirror image of each other. This is accentuated by the use of two different patterns bordered and defined by a cabled knit stitch. The body is knitted in reverse stocking stitch, while the first V is in moss stitch and the second is in rib emphasised by a centre knit stitch.

MATERIALS
13 (14) 50 gm balls thick-weight cotton
2 3 mm (11) needles
2 3¾ mm (9) needles
1 cable needle
1 3 mm (11) circular needle
stitch holders

MEASUREMENTS
Bust
small 89-91 cm (35-36 in)
medium 91-97 cm (36-38 in)
Approximate finished length to shoulder
small 74 cm (29 in)
medium 74 cm (29 in)

TENSION
24 sts and 33 rows for a 10 cm (4 in) square worked in st.st on 3¾ mm (9) needles

FRONT, BACK AND SLEEVES
Worked all in one. With 3 mm (11) needles cast on 110 (116) sts. Work 15 cm (6 in) in k2, p2 rib. Inc 1 st extra at the end of the last row. (111: 117) sts. Change to 3¾ mm (9) needles.

FIRST PART OF PATTERN
Work 44 rows in r.st.st inc 1 st at each end of 5th and evey following 12th row. (119: 125) sts.

SECOND PART OF PATTERN
1st row: with right side facing p 59 (62) sts, k1, p to end of row.
2nd row: k 59 (62) sts, p1, k to end of row.
3rd row: p 58 (61) sts, k1, p1, k1, p to end of row.

4th row: k 58 (61) sts, p1, k1, p1, k to end of row.
5th row: p 57 (60) sts, using cable needle sl.1B, k1, pss, k1, using cable needle sl.1F, p1, kss, p to end of row.
6th row: k 57 (60) sts, (p1, k1) 3 times, k to end of row.
7th row: p 56 (59) sts, sl.1B, k1, pss, k1, p1, k1, sl.1F, p1, kss, p to end of row.
8th row: k 56 (59) sts, (p1, k1) 4 times, k to end of row.
This sets the position of the pattern. Continue, increasing the V shape by 2 sts every p row, and keeping continuity correct when increasing on sides. When 48 rows have been worked the 2nd part of the pattern is complete. (127: 133) sts.

THIRD PART OF PATTERN
Divide for V neck and work sleeves
1st row: with right side facing cast on 4 sts, p 43 (46) sts, sl.1B, k1, pss, (k1, p1) 11 times. Turn and continue on these 67 (70) sts leaving remaining 64 (67) sts on a s.st.h. Continue working V-shape pattern outward by 1 st every p row while at the same time dec 1 st at neck edge every p row *and* casting on 4 sts at side edge every alt row (for sleeve). When 48 rows have been worked (136: 139) sts, continue working V neck and V pattern as set but work *straight* at side edge. Work 48 rows (112: 115) sts. These last 96 rows complete the 3rd part of the pattern. Mark the last row for shoulder. Now work 3rd part of pattern in reverse as follows:
next row: with right side facing p 88 (91) sts,

sl.1F, p1, kss, (p1, k1) 11 times, inc into last st. (113: 116) sts.

next row: (k1, p1) 12 times, k to end of row. Continue as set for a further 46 rows. (136: 139) sts. Now work 48 rows, dec for sleeve by casting off 4 sts at side edge every alternate row while inc at neck edge and keeping continuity of V shape and pattern correct. (63: 66) sts. Leave sts on a s.st.h.

NOW WORK OTHER HALF

Leaving the centre st on a s.st.h, rejoin yarn to remaining 63 (66) sts. Work to correspond to other side reversing shapings and pattern. Now work 2nd part of pattern in reverse joining the 2 halves to work straight across as follows: with right side facing, rejoin yarn and keeping continuity of pattern correct, work across one half of back, cast on 1 st then work across other half of back. (127: 133) sts. Continue working V pattern as set dec 1 st at each end of 3rd and every following 12th row until 48 rows have been completed. (119: 125) sts. Now work 1st part of pattern in reverse keeping continuity of side dec correct. When 44 rows of 1st part of pattern are complete (111: 117) sts, dec 1 st extra at the end of the next row. (110: 116) sts. Change to 3 mm (11) needles and work 15 cm

(6 in) in k2, p2 rib. Cast off loosely in rib.
Cuffs
Work 2 the same. With right side facing and 3 mm (11) needles, pick up and k 54 sts evenly along bottom edge of sleeve. Work 9 cm (3½ in) in k2, p2 rib. Cast off loosely in rib.
Neck edge
With right side facing and 3 mm (11) circular needle, start at shoulder point. Pick up and k 1 st at shoulder point, 85 sts down side edge, 1 st at centre point (either from s.st.h or cast on st), 85 sts up side edge, 1 st at shoulder point, 85 sts down side edge, 1 st at centre point, 85 sts up side edge. (344 sts). Work 27 rounds in k1, p1 rib as follows:

1st round: (k1, p1) for 84 sts, p2 tog tbl; k1, p2 tog, (p1, k1) for 166 sts, p1, p2 tog tbl, k1, p2 tog, (p1, k1) to last st, p1.

2nd and every following round: work in rib as set to 2 sts before centre st, p2 tog tbl, k1, p2 tog, rib as set to 2 sts before centre st, p2 tog tbl, k1, p2 tog, rib as set to complete round. Cast off in rib *not* loosely but also not *too* tightly. Neck edge must be held together by cast off row but not too obviously pulled in.

MAKING UP

Work in all ends, sew side and sleeve seams.

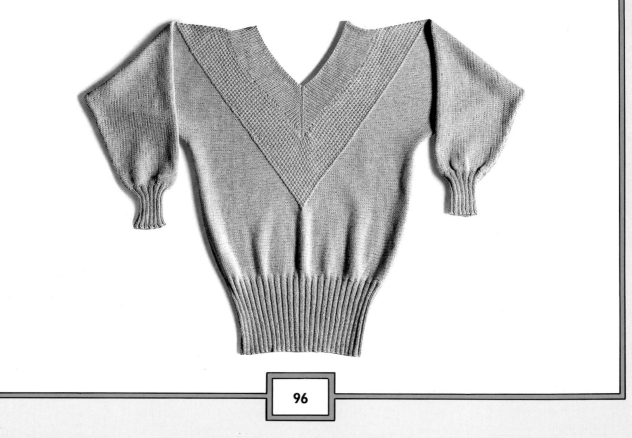

CLIFTON
Man's sweater in thick cotton

A chunky classic sweater patterned with traditional Guernsey style stitches. The body and sleeves are worked in reverse stocking stitch and the pattern starts with cables and purled diamonds either side of a central moss stitch panel. The round neck is in a rolled rib.

MATERIALS
14 (15: 15: 16) 50 gm balls thick-weight cotton
2 3 mm (11) needles
2 3¾ mm (9) needles
4 3 mm (11) double pointed needles
cable needle
stitch holders

MEASUREMENTS
Chest
97 (102: 107: 112) cm
38 (40: 42: 44) in
Measurement at widest point
117 (122: 127: 132) cm
46 (48: 50: 52) in
Length to shoulder
68 (69: 70: 71) cm
26½ (27: 27½: 28) in
Sleeve length
57 (59: 60: 60) cm
22½ (23: 23½: 23½) in

TENSION
25 sts and 33 rows for a 10 cm (4 in) square worked in pattern on 3¾ mm (9) needles

BACK
* With 3 mm (11) needles cast on 110 (116: 122: 128) sts. Work 9 cm (3½ in) in k2, p2 rib. Change to 3¾ mm (9) needles.
next row: with right side facing k 5 (8: 11: 14) sts, *k2, inc into next st; repeat from * to last 6 (9: 12: 15) sts, k to end of row. (143: 149: 155: 161) sts. Work 1 row p. Now continue in pattern as follows:
1st row: with right side facing p 14 (17: 20: 23) sts, (k4, p4) twice, k10, p1, k10, p4, work next

33 sts in moss st thus (k1, p1 to last st, k1), p4, k10, p1, k10, (p4, k4) twice, p to end of row.
2nd row: k 14 (17: 20: 23) sts, (p4, k4) twice, p9, k3, p9, k4, work next 33 sts in moss st thus (k1, p1 to last st, k1), k4, p9, k3, p9, (k4, p4) twice, k to end of row.
3rd row: p 14 (17: 20: 23) sts, (k4, p4) twice, k8, p5, k8, p4, work 33 sts in moss st, p4, k8, p5, k8, (p4, k4) twice, p to end of row.
4th row: k 14 (17: 20: 23) sts, (p4, k4) twice, p7, k7, p7, k4, work 33 sts in moss st, k4, p7, k7, p7, (k4, p4) twice, k to end of row.
5th row: p 14 (17: 20: 23) sts, (k4, p4) twice, k6, p9, k6, p4, work 33 sts in moss st, p4, k6, p9, k6, (p4, k4) twice, p to end of row.
6th row: k 14 (17: 20: 23) sts, (p4, k4) twice, p5, k11, p5, k4, work 33 sts in moss st, k4, p5, k11, p5, (k4, p4) twice, k to end of row.
7th row: p 14 (17: 20: 23) sts, cable next 4 sts thus: (put first 2 sts on a cable needle and leave at front of work, k2, k2 sts from cable needle, p4) twice, k4, p13, k4, p4, work 33 sts in moss st, p4, k4, p13, k4, (p4, cable next 4 sts) twice, p to end of row.
8th row: k 14 (17: 20: 23) sts, (p4, k4) twice, p3, k15, p3, k4, work 33 sts in moss st, k4, p3, k15, p3, (k4, p4) twice, k to end of row.
9th row: p 14 (17: 20: 23) sts, (k4, p4) twice, k2, p17, k2, p4, work 33 sts in moss st, p4, k2, p17, k2, (p4, k4) twice, p to end of row.
10th row: k 14 (17: 20: 23) sts, (p4, k4) twice, p1, k19, p1, k4, work 33 sts in moss st, k4, p1, k19, p1, (k4, p4) twice, k to end of row.
11th to 18th rows: now work backwards the pattern of the 9th to 2nd rows inclusive.
19th row: p 14 (17: 20: 23) sts, (cable next 4 sts, p4) twice, k10, p1, k10, p4, work 33 sts in

moss st, p4, k10, p1, k10, (p4, cable next 4 sts) twice, p to end of row.

These last 18 rows (2nd to 19th row) make the pattern. Continue repeating throughout keeping continuity correct. Continue straight until work measures 41 cm (16 in) from cast on edge.

turn and continue on these sts dec 1 st at neck edge every row until 38 (40: 42: 44) sts remain. Work 3 rows. Leave sts on s.st.h for shoulder seam. Leave centre 33 (35: 37: 39) sts on a s.st.h for neck edge. Rejoin yarn and work remaining 46 (48: 50: 52) sts to match other side.

Shape armholes

With right side facing work the first 9 sts and put them on a s.st.h, work to last 9 sts and put these on a s.st.h. Turn and continue on remaining 125 (131: 137: 143) sts. * Work straight for 75 (79: 83: 87) rows.

Shape neck

With right side facing work 46 (48: 50: 52) sts,

FRONT

Work the same as Back from * to *. Work straight for 57 (61: 65: 69) rows.

Shape neck

With right side facing work 46 (48: 50: 52) sts, turn and continue on these sts, dec 1 st at neck edge every row until 38 (40: 42: 44) sts remain. Work remaining rows (21 rows) to complete front to back length. Leave sts on a s.st.h. Put centre 33 (35: 37: 39) sts on a s.st.h for front neck edge. Rejoin yarn and continue on remaining 46 (48: 50: 52) sts. Work to match other side.

Shoulder seam

Work 2 the same. With 3¾ mm (9) needles put 38 (40: 42: 44) sts from the back and the same from the front on to spare needles. Place these 2 needles side by side with the wrong sides of work facing each other. Then working on the right side of work, k tog a st from each needle to give 1 st on right hand needle. *K tog the next 2 sts (now 2 sts on right hand needle) then pass the 1st of these 2 sts over the 2nd. Repeat from * to work the rest of the sts.

Neck edge

With right side facing and 4 3 mm (11) double pointed needles, pick up and k 1 st from shoulder seam, 10 sts down side back, 33 (35: 37: 39) sts from s.st.h, 10 sts up side back, 1 st from shoulder seam, 22 sts down side front, 33 (35: 37: 39) sts on s.st.h, 22 sts up side front.

(132: 136: 140: 144) sts. Work 16 rows in k1, p1 rib. Cast off loosely in rib. *Make sure a man will be able to get his head through.*

SLEEVES

Work 2 the same. With right side facing and 3¾ mm (9) needles pick up and k 9 sts from s.st.h (armhole shaping), 117 (123: 129: 135) sts evenly along armhole edge with centre st at shoulder seam and 9 sts on s.st.h. (135: 141: 147: 153) sts. Now work sleeve in r.st.st dec 1 st at each end of every 5th row until 73 (77: 81: 87) sts remain and work measures 48 (50: 51: 51) cm, 19 (19½: 20: 20) in.

Shape cuff

With wrong side facing dec 19 (21: 23: 27) sts evenly along the row. (54: 56: 58: 60) sts. Change to 3 mm (11) needles and work 9 cm (3½ in) in k2, p2 rib. Cast off loosely in rib.'

MAKING UP

Work in all ends, sew down rolled neck edge to inside of work, sew side and sleeve seams.

BADMINTON
Ladies jumper in fine cotton

A long slender shape for long summer days looking longer
still with its lines of moss stitch rib squared off prettily at the
neck with a buttoned moss stitch border.

MATERIALS
7 (8: 8: 9) 50 gm balls fine-weight cotton
2 2¼ mm (13) needles
2 pairs of 3 mm (11) needles
3 buttons 1.5 cm (½ in) diameter
stitch holders

MEASUREMENTS
87 (92: 97: 102) cm
34 (36: 38: 40) in
Measurement at widest point
102 (107: 112: 117) cm
40 (42: 44: 46) in
Finished length to shoulder
69: (70: 71: 72) cm
27 (27½: 28: 28½) in
Sleeve length
18 (18: 18: 18) cm
7 (7: 7: 7) in

TENSION
28 sts and 38 rows for a 10 cm (4 in) square
worked in pattern on 3 mm (11) needles

FRONT AND BACK
Knitted in one. With 2¼ mm (13) needles cast
on 124 (132: 140: 148) sts. Work 8 cm (3 in) in
k2, p2 rib. Change to 3 mm (11) needles.
next row: k0 (2: 6: 10) sts, *k7, inc into next st;
repeat from * to last 4 (10: 14: 18) sts, k to end
of row. (139: 147: 155: 163) sts. Now continue
straight in moss st rib as follows:
1st row: with wrong side facing, p.
2nd row: k5 (1: 5: 1) sts, (p1, k7) 8 (9: 9: 10)
times, p1,(k7, p1) 8 (9: 9: 10) times, k5 (1: 5: 1)
sts.
These two rows make 1 pattern. Repeat
throughout keeping continuity correct. When
work measures 47 cm (18½ in) from cast on
edge.

Shape armholes
With right side facing work the first 8 sts at the
beginning of the next 2 rows and put them on a
s.st.h. (123: 131: 139: 147) sts. Work straight
on these sts for 8 (10: 14: 18) rows.
next row: with right side facing work 38 (42:
46: 50) sts. Now continue on this row and cast
on 13 sts with 2¼ mm (13) needles. Turn and
continue on these sts leaving remaining 85 (89:
93: 97) sts on a s.st.h.
1st row: with 2¼ mm (13) needles work 13 sts
in moss st thus:
(p1, k1) to last st, p1 then with 3 mm (11)
needles p to end of row.
2nd row: with 3 mm (11) needles work to last
13 sts then with 2¼mm (13) needles work these
sts in moss st thus:
(p1, k1) to last st, p1.
Repeat these last 2 rows 14 more times.
Work square neck edge and shoulder
1st row: with wrong side facing and 2¼ mm
(13) needles work 26 sts in moss st, change to 3
mm (11) needles and p25 (29: 33: 37) sts.
2nd row: with 3 mm (11) needles work 25 (29:
33: 37) sts, change to 2¼ mm (13) needles and
work in moss st to end of row.
Repeat these last 2 rows 8 more times.
next row: with wrong side facing and 2¼ mm
(13) needles cast off 13 sts, work 13 sts in moss
st, change to 3mm (11) needles and p to end of
row. (38: 42: 46: 50) sts.
1st row: with 3 mm (11) needles work 25 (29:
33: 37) sts, change to 2¼ mm (13) needles and
work in moss st to end of row.
2nd row: with 2¼ mm (13) needles work 13 sts
in moss st, change to 3 mm (11) needles, p to
end of row.
Repeat these last 2 rows 20 more times. Leave
these sts on a s.st.h. Pick up the 85 (89: 93: 97)
sts on s.st.h, rejoin yarn and work other side as

follows:

To work buttonhole

With right side facing k 6 sts, yfwd, k2 tog, work to end of row.

next row: with right side facing and 2¼ mm (13) needles work 13 sts in moss st thus: (p1, k1) to the last st, p1, change to 3 mm (11) needles and work remaining 72 (76: 80: 84) sts.

and 29th rows.

Work square neck edge and shoulder

1st row: with right side facing and 2¼ mm (13) needles work 60 sts in moss st, change to 3 mm (11) needles and work 25 (29: 33: 37) sts to end of row.

2nd row: with 3 mm (11) needles p25 (29: 33: 37) sts, change to 2¼ mm (13) needles and

1st row: with wrong side facing and 3 mm (11) needles p to last 13 sts, change to 2¼ mm (13) needles and work in moss st to end of row thus: (p1, k1) to last st, p1.

2nd row: with 2¼ mm (13) needles work 13 sts in moss st, change to 3 mm (11) needles and work to end of row.

Repeat these last 2 rows until work corresponds to other side, *at the same time working 2 buttonholes into border* on the 15th

work in moss st to end of row.

Repeat these last 2 rows 8 more times and the first row once more, *at the same time working a buttonhole* on the 13th row.

next row: with wrong side facing and 3 mm (11) needles, p 25 (29: 33: 37) sts, change to 2¼ mm (13) needles and work 13 sts in moss st, cast off remaining 47 sts. (38: 42: 46: 50) sts. Rejoin yarn to these sts and work to match other side.

Join shoulders for back neck edge

next row: with wrong side facing and 3 mm (11) needles p25 (29: 33: 37) sts, change to 2¼ mm (13) needles and work 13 sts in moss st then cast on 47 sts then work 13 sts in moss st from s.st.h (other shoulder), change to 3 mm (11) needles and p to end of row. (123: 131: 139: 147) sts.

1st row: with 3 mm (11) needles work 25 (29: 33: 37) sts, change to 2¼ mm (13) needles and work 73 sts in moss st, change to 3 mm (11) needles and work to end of row.

2nd row: with 3 mm (11) needles p 25 (29: 33: 37) sts, change to 2¼ mm (13) needles and work 73 sts in moss st, change to 3 mm (11) needles and p to end of row.

Repeat these last 2 rows 8 more times. Change to 3 mm (11) needles and continue straight in moss st rib for 56 (60: 64: 68) rows.

Shape armholes

Cast on 8 sts at the beg of the next 2 rows (139: 147: 155: 163) sts. Now continue straight until back corresponds to front length.

Shape to welt

With wrong side facing p0 (2: 6: 10) sts, *p7, p2 tog; repeat from *to last 4 (10: 14: 18) sts, p to end of row. (124: 132: 140: 148) sts. Change to 2¼ mm (13) needles and work 8 cm (3 in) in k2, p2 rib. Cast off loosely in rib.

SLEEVES

Work 2 the same. With right side facing and 3 mm (11) needles, pick up and k 8 sts from s.st.h (armhole shaping), 117 (125: 133: 141) sts evenly along armhole edge and 8 sts from armhole shaping. (133: 141: 149: 157) sts.

next row: p

Now work in moss st rib working the pattern row thus:

k2 (6: 2: 6) sts, (p1, k7) 8 (8: 9: 9) times, p1, (k7, p1) 8 (8: 9: 9) times, k remaining 2 (6: 2: 6) sts. Continue in pattern keeping continuity correct, dec 1 st at each end of every alternate row until 85 (93: 101: 109) sts remain and work measures 14 cm (5½ in).

Shape to cuff

With wrong side facing p1 (5: 9: 13) sts, *p2 tog, p2; repeat from * to last 0 (4: 8: 12) sts, p to end of row. 64 (72: 80: 88) sts. Change to 2¼ mm (13) needles and work 4 cm (1½ in) in k2, p2 rib. Cast off in rib.

MAKING UP

Work in all ends. Sew bottom edge of button border to inside of front opening (take care to do this neatly), buttons to corresponding positions to buttonholes. Sew throughout the side and sleeve seams from welt to cuff.

GRAMPA
Ladies jumper in thick cotton

This jumper is based on a shape very close to grandfather's heart. Although it is simple and looks good worn in a sporty way it can also look surprisingly dressy with pearls or a lace scarf. The buttonhole bands, pocket top and welts are worked in twisted rib, the rest of the jumper in stocking stitch.

MATERIALS
11 (12: 13: 14) 50 gm balls thick-weight cotton
2 3 mm (11) needles
2 3¾ mm (9) needles
stitch holders
3 buttons 1.5 cm (½ in) diameter

MEASUREMENTS
Bust
87 (92: 97: 102) cm
34 (36: 38: 40) in
Actual measurement
100 (105: 110: 115) cm
39½ (41½: 43½: 45½) in
Finished length to shoulder
69 (70: 71: 72) cm
27 (27½: 28: 28½) in
Sleeve length
50 (51: 52: 52) cm
19½ (20: 20½: 20½) in

TENSION
24 sts and 33 rows for a 10 cm (4 in) square worked in st.st on 3¾ mm (9) needles

BACK
*With 3 mm (11) needles cast on 108 (114: 120: 126) sts. Work 9 cm (3½ in) in k2, p2 rib. Change to 3¾ mm (9) needles and continue in st.st working 1st row as follows:
k 8 (11: 14: 17) sts, * inc into next st, k8; repeat from * to last 1 (4: 7: 10) sts, k to end of row. (119: 125: 131: 137) sts. Continue straight until work measures 44 cm (17½ in) from cast on edge.*
Shape armholes
With right side facing

next row: k the first 8 sts and put them on a s.st.h, k to last 8 sts and put these on a s.st.h. Turn and continue on remaining 103 (109: 115: 121) sts. Work a further 65 (69: 73: 77) rows.
Shape neck
With right side facing
next row: k 47 (49: 51: 53) sts, turn and continue on these sts dec 1 st at neck edge *every* row as follows:
on p rows: p2, p2 tog, p to end of row.
on k rows: k to last 4 sts, k2 tog, k2
until 34 (36: 38: 40) sts remain. Leave sts on a s.st.h for shoulder seams and 9 (11: 13: 15) sts at centre (back neck edge) on a s.st.h. Rejoin yarn and continue on remaining 47 (49: 51: 53) sts. Work to match other side reversing shapings and working dec rows as follows:
on p rows: p to last 4 sts, p2 tog tbl, p2.
on k rows: k2, sl.1, k1, psso, k to end of row.
Pocket lining
With 3¾ mm (9) needles cast on 21 sts and work 10 cm (4 in) in st.st. Leave sts on a s.st.h.

FRONT
Work the same as Back from * to *.
Shape armhole, place pocket lining, divide for front opening
With right side facing
next row: k the first 8 sts and put them on a s.st.h, k 16 sts, slip next 21 sts on to a s.st.h and in place of these k across 21 sts of pocket lining, k 10 (13: 16: 19) sts, turn and continue on these 47 (50: 53: 56) sts. Work straight for 33 (37: 41: 45) rows.
Shape neck
With right side facing
next row: k 43 (45: 47: 49) sts, leave remaining

4 (5: 6: 7) sts on a s.st.h for neck edge, turn and continue on remaining sts decreasing 1 st at neck edge on every k row as follows:
k to last 4 sts, k2 tog, k2 until 34 (36: 38: 40) sts remain.
Work straight for a further 28 rows when the front will measure the same as the back. Leave sts on a s.st.h for shoulder seam, leave centre 9

pick up and rib on man's side in k1, p1 twisted rib (k into back of k sts) the 9 sts on s.st.h as follows:
1st row: k2, *p1, k1; repeat from * to last st, k1.
2nd row: k1, *p1, k1; repeat from * to end of row.
Repeat these 2 rows to work border working 2 buttonholes spaced evenly so that a 3rd

sts on a s.st.h for front opening and continue on remaining 55 (58: 61: 64) sts. Work to match other side of front omitting the pocket and working dec rows as follows:
k2, sl.1, k1, psso, k to end of row.
To work buttonhole
With right side facing work 4 sts, yarn round needle, k2 tog, work rest of row.

FRONT BORDERS
Buttonhole border
With right side facing and 3 mm (11) needles,

buttonhole will be in neck edge. *Border must be 1 cm (½ in) shorter than front edge.* Leave sts on a s.st.h.
Button border
With 3 mm (11) needles cast on 9 sts. Work border in k1, p1 twisted rib to correspond to buttonhole border. Leave sts on s.st.h.
Shoulder seam
Work 2 the same. With 3¾ mm (9) needles put 34 (36: 38: 40) sts from the back and the same from the front on to spare needles. Place these 2 needles side by side with the wrong sides of

work facing each other. Then working on the right side of work, k tog a st from each needle to give 1 st on right hand needle. *K tog the next 2 sts (now 2 sts on right hand needle) then pass the 1st of these 2 sts over the 2nd. Repeat from * to work the rest of the sts.

Neck edge

With right side facing and 3 mm (11) needles, start at button border. Rib across 9 sts of button border, k across 4 (5: 6: 7) sts on s.st.h (front neck edge), pick up and k 34 sts up side front, 1 st at shoulder seam, 13 sts down side back, 9 (11: 13: 15) sts on s.st.h, 13 sts up side back, 1 st at shoulder seam, 34 sts down side front, 4 (5: 6: 7) sts on s.st.h and rib across 9 sts of buttonhole border. (131: 135: 139: 143) sts. Work 7 rows in k1, p1 twisted rib, working a buttonhole on the 4th row. Cast off in rib.

Pocket top

With 3 mm (11) needles pick up and k 21 sts from s.st.h. Work 7 rows in k1, p1 twisted rib. Cast off in rib.

SLEEVES

Work 2 the same. With right side facing and 3¾ mm (9) needles pick up and k 8 sts from s.st.h (armhole shaping), 109 (115: 121: 127) sts evenly along armhole edge with centre stitch at shoulder seam and 8 sts from s.st.h. (125: 131: 137: 143) sts. Now work in st.st decreasing 1 st at each end of every 4th row as follows:
k2, sl.1, k1, psso, k to last 4 sts, k2 tog, k2. until 59 (63: 67: 73) sts remain.

Shape cuff

With wrong side facing dec 15 (17: 19: 23) sts evenly along row. (44: 46: 48: 50) sts. Change to 3 mm (11) needles and work 9 cm (3½ in) in k2, p2 rib. Cast off loosely in rib.

MAKING UP

Work in all ends. Sew front bands to fronts, pocket top edges to front, pocket lining to inside of work, sew side and sleeve seams and buttons to border as marked.

RUGGER
Sweater for men and women in thick cotton

A spectator classic, two versions of the same sporty sweater. The ladies' version is long and lean with a garter stitch collar on a ribbed stand neck, while the man's version is broad, shorter in proportion and with a rolled rib crew neck. The design has classic Guernsey origins with chains of diamond shapes divided by ladders.

MATERIALS
Ladies
14 (14: 15) gm balls thick-weight cotton
Men
14 (15: 16) 50 gm balls thick-weight cotton
2 3 mm (11) needles
2 3¾ mm (9) needles
4 3 mm (11) double pointed needles
stitch holders

MEASUREMENTS
Bust
92 (97: 102) cm
36 (38: 40) in
Chest
97 (102: 107) cm
38 (40: 42) in
Measurement at widest point
Ladies
107 (112: 117) cm
42 (44: 46) in
Men
117 (122: 127) cm
46 (48: 50) in
Finished length to shoulder
Ladies
70 (71: 72) cm
27½ (28: 28½) in
Men
67 (68: 70) cm
26½ (27: 27½) in
Sleeve length
Ladies
53 (54: 55) cm
21 (21½: 22) in

Men
57 (58: 59) cm
22½ (23: 23½) in

TENSION
25 sts and 33 rows for a 10 cm (4 in) square worked in pattern on 3¾ mm (9) needles

BACK
With 3 mm (11) needles cast on (**ladies**) 114 (120: 126) sts, (**men**) 110 (116: 122) sts. Work 9 cm (3½ in) in k2, p2 rib. Change to 3¾ mm (9) needles.
Ladies 1st row: k 3 (6: 9) sts, * k5, inc into next st; repeat from * to last 9 (12: 15) sts, k to end of row.
Men 1st row: k 5 (8: 11) sts, * k2, inc into next st; repeat from * to last 6 (9: 12) sts, k to end of row.
(**ladies**) (131: 137: 143) sts, (**men**) (143: 149: 155) sts.
2nd row: p.
Now work in diamond and stripe pattern as follows with right side facing. Until armhole shaping is reached work beginning and end of rows thus:
Ladies 92 cm (36 in) on k rows: k3, p2, k4, p2 and end with p2, k4, p2, k3.
on p rows: beg with p11 and end with p11.
Ladies 97 cm (38 in) on k rows: p2, (k4, p2) twice end with (p2, k4) twice, p2.
on p rows: beg with p14 and end with p14.
Ladies 102 cm (40 in) on k rows: k3, p2, (k4, p2) twice end with (p2, k4) twice, p2, k3.
on p rows: beg with p17 and end with p17.
Men 97 cm (38 in) on k rows: k3, p2, (k4, p2)

twice end with (p2, k4) twice, p2, k3.

on p rows: beg with p17 and end with p17.
Men 102 cm (40 in) on k rows: p2, (k4, p2) 3 times end with (p2, k4) 3 times, p2.
on p rows: beg with p20 and end with p20.
Men 107 cm (42 in) on k rows: k3, p2, (k4, p2) 3 times end with (p2, k4) 3 times, p2, k3.
on p rows: beg with p23 and end with p23.

4th row: p17, (k1, p1) 9 times, p18, (k1, p1) twice, p18, (k1, p1) 9 times, p16.
5th row: (k4, p2) twice, k6, (p1, k1) 8 times, k5, p2, k11, (p1, k1) 3 times, k10, p2, k6, (p1, k1) 8 times, k5, (p2, k4) twice.
6th row: p18, (k1, p1) 8 times, p18, (k1, p1) 3 times, p18, (k1, p1) 8 times, p17.

These last 6 rows set the pattern. Continue as

PATTERN

With right side facing

1st row: (k4, p2) twice, k4, (p1, k1) 10 times, k3, p2, k13, p1, k13, p2, k4, (p1, k1) 10 times, (p2, k4) twice.
2nd row: p16, (k1, p1) 10 times, p18, k1, p19, (k1, p1) 10 times, p15.
3rd row: (k4, p2) twice, k5, (p1, k1) 9 times, k4, p2, k12, (p1, k1) twice, k11, p2, k5, (p1, k1) 9 times, k4, (p2, k4) twice.

set inc and dec the moss st diamonds by 2 sts every k row as shown in the graph. Work 20 rows in all. Now work pattern in reverse as follows:

21st row: work 17th row.
22nd row: work 18th row.
23rd row: work 15th row.
24th row: work 16th row.
25th row: work 13th row.
26th row: work 14th row.

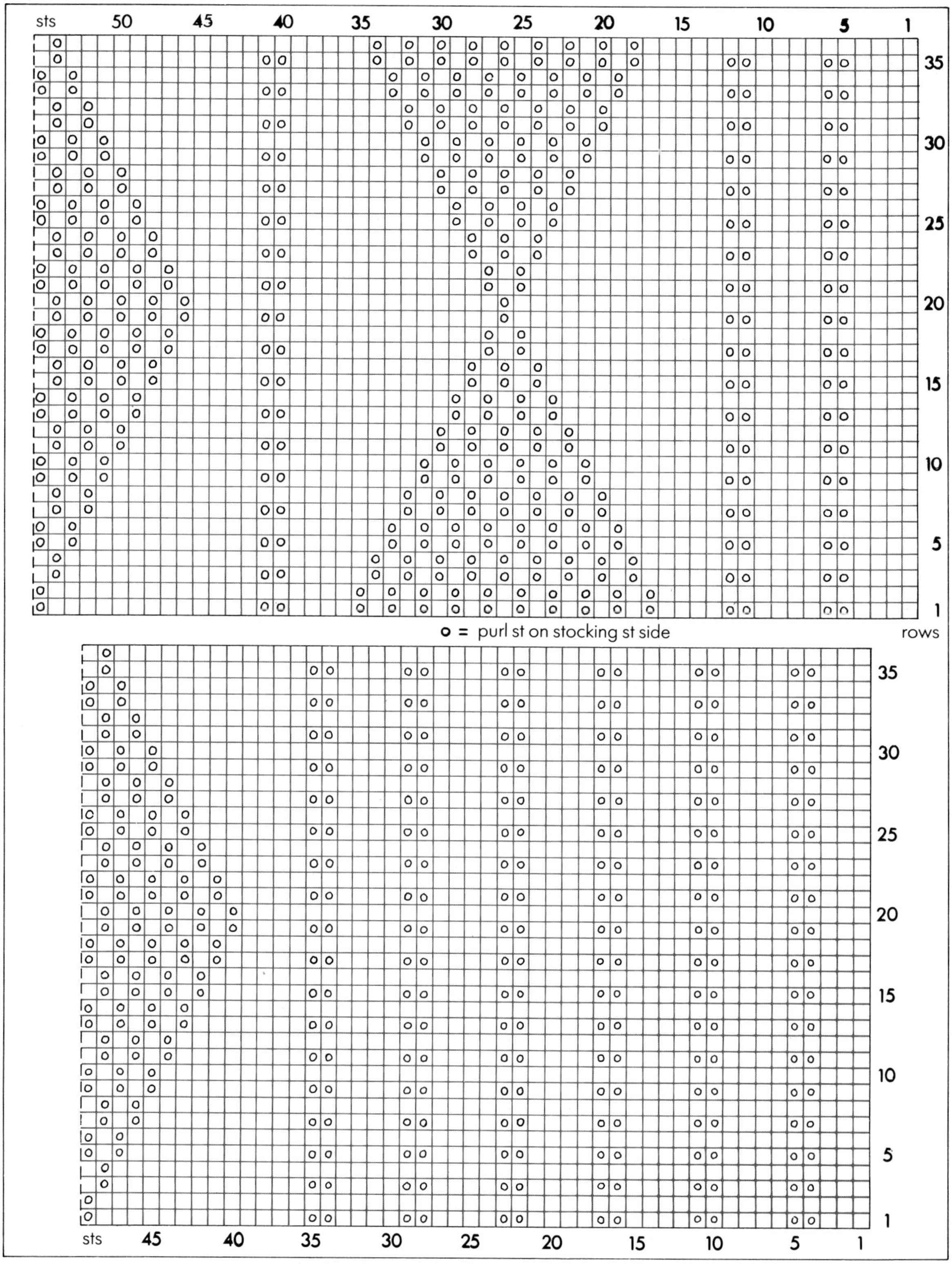

sts 50 45 40 35 30 25 20 15 10 5 1

35

30

25

20

15

10

5

1

o = purl st on stocking st side rows

sts 45 40 35 30 25 20 15 10 5 1

35

30

25

20

15

10

5

1

Graphs of patterning on body (above) and sleeves (below)

These last 6 rows set the pattern. Continue as set dec and inc the moss st diamonds by 2 sts every k row. When 36 rows have been worked in all, one pattern is complete. Continue working in pattern throughout keeping continuity correct. When work measures (**ladies**) 43 cm (17in) from cast on edge, (**men**) 42 cm (16½ in) from cast on edge

Shape armholes

With right side facing

Ladies: k the first 8 sts and put these sts on a s.st.h, work to the last 8 sts and put these on a s.st.h.

Men: k the first 9 sts and put these sts on a s.st.h, work to the last 9 sts and put these on a s.st.h. Turn and continue on remaining

Ladies: 115 (121: 127) sts * and continue straight for 87 (91: 95) rows. Leave all sts on a s.st.h for shoulder seams and neck edge.

Men: 125 (131: 137) sts * and continue straight for 75 (79: 83) rows. With right side facing work 46 (48: 50) sts, turn and continue on these sts dec 1 st at neck edge every row until 38 (40: 42) sts remain. Work 3 more rows and leave sts on a s.st.h for shoulder seam. Leave centre 33 (35: 37) sts on a s.st.h for neck edge. Rejoin yarn and continue on remaining 46 (48: 50) sts and work to match other side.

FRONT

Work the same as Back from * to *. Continue straight for

Ladies: 51 (55: 59) rows.

Shape neck

With right side facing work 49 (51: 53) sts, turn and continue on these sts dec 1 st at neck edge every row until 40 (42: 44) sts remain. Continue straight for 26 rows or until work corresponds to back length. Leave sts on a s.st.h for shoulder seam. Leave centre 17 (19: 21) sts on a s.st.h for neck edge. Rejoin yarn and continue on remaining 49 (51: 53) sts. Work to match other side of front, reversing shaping.

Men: 57 (61: 65) rows.

Shape neck

With right side facing work 46 (48: 50) sts, turn and continue on these sts dec 1 st at neck edge every row until 38 (40: 42) sts remain. Continue straight for 21 rows or until work corresponds to back length. Leave sts on a s.st.h for shoulder seam. Leave centre 33 (35: 37) sts on

a s.st.h for neck edge. Rejoin yarn and continue on remaining 46 (48: 50) sts. Work to match other side of front, reversing shaping.

Shoulder seam

Work 2 the same. With 3¾ mm (9) needles put

Ladies: 40 (42: 44) sts

Men: 38 (40: 42) sts

from the back and the same from the front on to spare needles. Place these 2 needles side by side with the wrong sides of work facing each other. Then working on the right side of work, k tog a st from each needle to give 1 st on right hand needle. *K tog the next 2 sts (now 2 sts on right hand needle) then pass the 1st of these 2 sts over the 2nd. Repeat from * to work the rest of the sts.

COLLAR AND NECK EDGE (Ladies)

With right side facing and 4 3 mm (11) double pointed needles, start at centre front. Pick up and k from s.st.h (front neck edge) 9 (10: 11) sts, 27 sts up side front, 1 st at shoulder seam, 35 (37: 39) sts from s.st.h (back neck edge), 1 st at shoulder seam, 27 sts down side front and 8 (9: 10) sts from s.st.h. (108: 112: 116) sts. Work 8 rounds in k1, p1 rib. Now divide for collar. At centre front turn and now working in rows, work 8 cm (3 in) in g.st.
Cast off from *under* side of the collar.

NECK EDGE (Men)

With right side facing and 4 3 mm (11) double pointed needles, start at shoulder seam. Pick up and k 1st at shoulder seam, 10 sts down side back, 33 (35: 37) sts on s.st.h (back neck edge), 10 sts up side back, 1 st at shoulder seam, 21 sts down side front, 33 (35: 37) sts on s.st.h (front neck edge) and 21 sts up side front. (130: 134: 138) sts. Work 16 rounds in k1, p1 rib. Cast off in rib.

SLEEVES

Work 2 the same. With right side facing and 3¾ mm (9) needles pick up and k

Ladies: 8 sts from s.st.h, 121 (127: 133) sts evenly along armhole edge with centre stitch at shoulder seam and 8 sts from s.st.h. 137 (143: 149) sts.
Work 1 row p.

Men: 9 sts from s.st.h, 123 (129: 135) sts evenly along armhole edge with centre stitch at shoulder seam and 9 sts from s.st.h. (141: 147: 153) sts.

Work 1 row p.

Now work in diamond and stripe pattern as follows with right side facing, and *at the same time* dec 1 st at each end of (**ladies**) every 4th row, (**men**) every 5th row.

Decreasing is not accounted for.

Start the beginning and end of rows before working set pattern thus:

Ladies 92 cm (36 in) on k rows: p1, (k4, p2) 3 times, k1 end with k1, (p2, k4) 3 times, p1.

on p rows: beg with p 20 and end with p 20.

Ladies 97 cm (38 in) on k rows: k2, p2, (k4, p2) 3 times, k1 end with k1, (p2, k4) 3 times, p2, k2.

on p rows: beg with p23 and end with p23.

Ladies 102 cm (40 in) on k rows: p1, (k4, p2) 4 times, k1 end with k1, (p2, k4) 4 times, p1.

on p rows: beg with p26 and end with p26.

Men 97 cm (38 in) on k rows: k1, p2, (k4, p2) 3 times, k1 end with k1, (p2, k4) 3 times, p2, k1.

on p rows: beg with p22 and end with p22.

Men 102 cm (40 in) on k rows: (k4, p2) 4 times, k1 end with k1, (p2, k4) 4 times.

on p rows: beg with p25 and end with p25.

Men 107 cm (42 in) on k rows: k1, p2, (k4, p2) 4 times, k1 end with k1, (p2, k4) 4 times, p2, k1.

on p rows: beg with p28 and end with p28.

PATTERN

With right side facing

1st row: k3, p2, (k4, p2) 5 times, k13, p1, k13, (p2, k4) 5 times, p2, k3.

2nd row: p48, k1, p48.

3rd row: k3, p2, (k4, p2) 5 times, k12, p1, k1, p1, k12, (p2, k4) 5 times, p2, k3.

4th row: p47, k1, p1, k1, p47.

5th row: k3, p2, (k4, p2) 5 times, k11, (p1, k1) 3 times, k10, (p2, k4) 5 times, p2, k3.

6th row: p46, (k1, p1) 3 times, p45.

These last 6 rows set the pattern. Continue as set inc the moss st diamond by 2 sts every k row. Work 20 rows in all. Now work pattern in reverse as follows:

21st row: work 17th row.

22nd row: work 18th row.

23rd row: work 15th row.

24th row: work 16th row.

25th row: work 13th row.

26th row: work 14th row.

These last 6 rows set the pattern. Continue as set dec the moss st diamond by 2 sts every k row. When 36 rows have been worked, one pattern is complete. Continue working pattern throughout keeping continuity correct over dec until (**ladies**) 65 (69: 73) sts remain, (**men**) 79 (83: 87) sts remain.

Shape cuff

With wrong side facing dec evenly across row (**ladies**) 17 (19: 21) sts. 48 (50: 52) sts remain, (**men**) 25 (27: 29) sts. 54 (56: 58) sts remain. Change to 3 mm (11) needles and work 9 cm (3½ in) in k2, p2 rib. Cast off loosely in rib.

MAKING UP

Work in all ends, sew side and sleeve seams. For ladies' version, work a neat strengthening st at the inside of centre front neck where the collar divides. For men's version, sew rolled edge to inside of work.

CROQUET
Ladies jumper in fine cotton

A long summer sweater reminiscent of those days when croquet and cucumber sandwiches were part of a sunny afternoon. The body is worked in stocking stitch with a delicate lace pattern at the front and a square cut neck in moss stitch.

MATERIALS
10 (10: 11: 11) 50 gm balls fine-weight cotton
2 2¼ mm (13) needles
2 pairs 3 mm (11) needles
stitch holders

MEASUREMENTS
Bust
87 (92: 97: 102) cm
34 (36: 38: 40) in
Measurement at widest point
102 (107: 112: 117) cm
40 (42: 44: 46) in
Finished length to shoulder
68 (69: 70: 71) cm
27 (27½: 28: 28½) in
Sleeve length
50 (50: 50: 50) cm
19½ (19½: 19½: 19½) in

TENSION
28 sts and 38 rows for a 10 cm (4 in) square worked in st.st. on 3 mm (11) needles

FRONT AND BACK
Knitted in one. With 2¼ mm (13) needles cast on 124 (132: 140: 148) sts. Work 8 cm (3 in) in k2, p2 rib. Change to 3 mm (11) needles.
next row: k 0 (2: 6: 10) sts, *k7, inc into next st; repeat from * to last 4 (10: 14: 18) sts, k to end of row. (139: 147: 155: 163) sts. Now continue straight in s.st. When work measures 29 (30: 31: 32) cm 11½ (12: 12½: 13) in from cast on edge work 1st part of pattern as follows:
1st row: with right side facing k 69 (73: 77: 81) sts, yfwd, k2 tog, k 68 (72: 76: 80) sts.
2nd, 3rd and 4th rows: work in st.st.

5th row: k 67 (71: 75: 79) sts, yfwd, k2 tog, k2, yfwd, k2 tog, k 66 (70: 74: 78) sts.
6th, 7th and 8th rows: work in st.st.
9th row: k 65 (69: 73: 77) sts, yfwd, k2 tog, k6, yfwd, k2 tog, k 64 (68: 72: 76) sts.
10th, 11th and 12th rows: work in st.st.
13th row: k 63 (67: 71: 75) sts, yfwd, k2 tog, k10, yfwd, k2 tog, k 62 (66: 70: 74) sts.
14th, 15th and 16th rows: work in st.st.
17th row: k 61 (65: 69: 73) sts, yfwd, k2 tog, k 14, yfwd, k2 tog, k 60 (64: 68: 72) sts.
18th to 32nd rows: work backwards from 16th to 2nd rows inclusive.
These last 32 rows make the first part of the pattern. Now work 2nd part as follows:
1st row: k 47 (51: 55: 59) sts, (yfwd, k2 tog, k9) 4 times, yfwd, k2 tog, k 46 (50: 54: 58) sts.
2nd, 3rd and 4th rows: work in st.st.
5th row: k 45 (49: 53: 57) sts, (yfwd, k2 tog, k2, yfwd, k2 tog, k7, yfwd, k2 tog, k7) twice, yfwd, k2 tog, k2, yfwd, k2 tog, k 44 (48: 52: 56) sts.
6th, 7th and 8th rows: work in st.st.
9th row: k 43 (47: 51: 55) sts, (yfwd, k2 tog, k6, yfwd, k2 tog, k5, yfwd, k2 tog, k5) twice, yfwd, k2 tog, k6, yfwd, k2 tog, k 42 (46: 50: 54) sts.
10th, 11th and 12th rows: work in st.st.
13th row: k 41 (45: 49: 53) sts, (yfwd, k2 tog, k10, yfwd, k2 tog, k3, yfwd, k2 tog, k3) twice, yfwd, k2 tog, k10, yfwd, k2 tog, k 40 (44: 48: 52) sts.
14th, 15th, 16th and 18th rows: work in st.st.
17th row: k 39 (43: 47: 51) sts, (yfwd, k2 tog, k14, yfwd, k2 tog, k1, yfwd, k2 tog, k1) twice, yfwd, k2 tog, k14, yfwd, k2 tog, k 38 (42: 46: 50) sts.
Shape armholes
19th row: With right side facing k the first 9 sts

and put them on a s.st.h, k to last 9 sts, put them on a s.st.h. Turn and continue on remaining 121 (129: 137: 145) sts.

20th to 32nd rows: work backwards from 14th to 2nd rows inclusive taking into account that there will be 9 sts less at either end.

Now work 3rd part of pattern as follows:

1st row: k 27 (31: 35: 39) sts, (yfwd, k2 tog, k9)

13th row: k 27 (31: 35: 39) sts, (yfwd, k2 tog, k3, yfwd, k2 tog, k10, yfwd, k2 tog, k3) 3 times, yfwd, k2 tog, k 26 (30: 34: 38) sts.

14th, 15th and 16th rows: work in st.st.

17th row: k 27 (31: 35: 39) sts, (yfwd, k2 tog, k1, yfwd, k2 tog, k14, yfwd, k2 tog, k1) 3 times, yfwd, k2 tog, k26 (30: 34: 38) sts.

18th to 32nd rows: work backwards from 16th

6 times, yfwd, k2 tog, k 26 (30: 34: 38) sts.

2nd, 3rd and 4th rows: work in st.st.

5th row: k 27 (31: 35: 39) sts, (yfwd, k2 tog, k7, yfwd, k2 tog, k2, yfwd, k2 tog, k7) 3 times, yfwd, k2 tog, k 26 (30: 34: 38) sts.

6th, 7th and 8th rows: work in st.st.

9th row: k 27 (31: 35: 39) sts, (yfwd, k2 tog, k5, yfwd, k2 tog, k6, yfwd, k2 tog, k5) 3 times, yfwd, k2 tog, k 26 (30: 34: 38) sts.

10th, 11th and 12th rows: work in st.st.

to 2nd rows inclusive.

These last 32 rows make the 3rd part of the pattern.

next row: work 1st row of 3rd part of pattern. Now work 3 rows in st.st. This completes the 3 parts of the pattern.

Work square neck and shoulders

With right side facing

1st row: k 24 (28: 32: 36) sts then with 2¼ mm (13) needles work 73 sts in moss st thus: (p1,

k1) to last st, p1, then with 3 mm (11) needles, k remaining 24 (28: 32: 36) sts.
2nd row: With 3 mm (11) needles p 24 (28: 32: 36) sts, with 2¼ mm (13) needles work 73 sts in moss st thus: (p1, k1) to last st, p1, with 3 mm (11) needles p remaining 24 (28: 32: 36) sts. Repeat these two rows 8 more times. Now work 1st row once more.

Divide for shoulders
With wrong side facing
next row: with 3 mm (11) needles p 24 (28: 32: 36) sts, with 2¼ mm (13) needles work 13 sts in moss st and leave all these sts on a s.st.h. With 2¼ mm (13) needles cast off the next 47 sts and work 13 sts in moss st, with 3 mm (11) needles p 24 (28: 32: 36) sts.
1st row: With 3 mm (11) needles k 24 (28: 32: 36) sts, with 2¼ mm (13) needles work 13 sts in moss st.
2nd row: with 2¼ mm (13) needles work 13 sts in moss st, with 3 mm (11) needles p 24 (28: 32: 36) sts.
Repeat these last 2 rows for 39 rows finishing on a k row. Leave sts on a s.st.h. Pick up the 37 (41: 45: 49) sts on earlier s.st.h and work to correspond to other shoulder.
next row: with wrong side facing and 3 mm (11) needles p 24 (28. 32: 36) sts, with 2¼ mm (13) needles work 13 sts in moss st then cast on 47 sts and work 13 sts in moss st from s.st.h, with 3 mm (11) needles p the remaining 24 (28: 32: 36) sts. (121: 129: 137: 145) sts.
1st row: With 3 mm (11) needles k 24 (28: 32: 36) sts, with 2¼ mm (13) needles work 73 sts in moss st, with 3 mm (11) needles k 24 (28: 32: 36) sts.
2nd row: With 3 mm (11) needles p 24 (28: 32: 36) sts, with 2¼ mm (13) needles work 73 sts in moss st, with 3 mm (11) needles p to end of row. Repeat these last 2 rows 8 more times. At this point make sure you can get your head through. Now continue in st.st on 3 mm (11) needles for 74 rows.

Shape armholes
Cast on 9 sts at the end of the next 2 rows. (139: 147: 155: 163) sts. Now continue straight until back corresponds to front length before rib is worked.

Shape to welt
With wrong side facing p 0 (2: 6: 10) sts, *p7, p2 tog; repeat from * to last 4 (10: 14: 18) sts, p to end of row. (124: 132: 140: 148) sts. Change to 2¼ mm (13) needles and work 8 cm (3 in) in k2, p2 rib. Cast off in rib.

SLEEVES
Work 2 the same. With right side facing and 3 mm (11) needles pick up and k9 sts (armhole shaping), 147 sts evenly along armhole edge and 9 sts (armhole shaping). 165 sts. Now dec 1 st at each end of every 4th row as follows: k2, sl.1, k1, psso, k to last 4 sts, k2 tog, k2 until 87 sts remain.

Shape cuff
With wrong side facing dec 27 sts evenly along row. (60 sts.) Change to 2¼ mm (13) needles and work 8 cm (3 in) in k2, p2 rib. Cast off in rib.

MAKING UP
Work in all ends. Sew side and sleeve seams.

SPRINT
Ladies vest in fine cotton

This vest was inspired by an old fashioned knitted vest.
Simple and close fitting in shape, the fine details add interest.
Knitted in stocking stitch, with graduated lacy diamonds on
the front and edged with garter stitch round the neckline and
armholes.

MATERIALS
6 (7) 50 gm balls fine-weight cotton
2 2¼ mm (13) needles
2 3 mm (11) needles
stitch holders

MEASUREMENTS
Bust
small 84-89 cm (33-35 in)
medium 92-96 cm (36-38 in)
Actual measurement
89 (96) cm
35 (38) in
Finished length to shoulder
71 (71) cm
28 (28) in

TENSION
28 sts and 38 rows for a 10 cm (4 in) square
worked in st.st on 3 mm (11) needles

FRONT AND BACK
Knitted in one. With 2¼ mm (13) needles cast
on 124 (132) sts. Work 8 cm (3 in) in k2, p2 rib,
inc 1 st extra at the end of the last row. (125:
133) sts. Change to 3 mm (11) needles and
continue in st.st. Work straight until work
measures 22 cm (8½ in) from cast on edge.
Now work 1st part of pattern as follows:
1st row: with right side facing k 62 (66) sts,
yfwd, k2 tog, k 61 (65) sts.
2nd, 3rd and 4th rows: work in st.st.
Repeat these last 4 rows 2 more times. Now
work 2nd part of pattern as follows:
1st row: k 62 (66), yfwd, k2 tog, k 61 (65).
2nd, 3rd and 4th rows: work in st.st.
5th row: k 60 (64) sts, yfwd, k2 tog, k2, yfwd, k2

tog, k 59 (63) sts.
6th, 7th and 8th rows: work in st.st.
9th row: k 58 (62) sts, yfwd, k2 tog, k6, yfwd, k2
tog, k 57 (61) sts.
10th, 11th and 12th rows: work in st.st.
13th row: k 56 (60) sts, yfwd, k2 tog, k10, yfwd,
k2 tog, k 55 (59) sts.
14th, 15th and 16th rows: work in st.st.
17th row: k 54 (58) sts, yfwd, k2 tog, k14, yfwd,
k2 tog, k 53 (57) sts.
18th to 32nd rows: work backwards from the
16th to 2nd row inclusive.
These last 32 rows make the 2nd part of the
pattern. Now work the 3rd part of the pattern
as follows:
1st row: k 62 (66) sts, yfwd, k2 tog, k 61 (65)
sts.
2nd, 3rd and 4th rows: work in st.st.
5th row: k 60 (64) sts, yfwd, k2 tog, k2, yfwd, k2
tog, k 59 (63) sts.
6th, 7th and 8th rows: work in st.st.
9th row: k 58 (62) sts, yfwd, k2 tog, k6, yfwd, k2
tog, k 57 (61) sts.
10th, 11th and 12th rows: work in st.st.
13th row: k 56 (60) sts, yfwd, k2 tog, k10, yfwd,
k2 tog, k 55 (59) sts.
14th, 15th and 16th rows: work in st.st.
17th row: k 54 (58) sts, yfwd, k2 tog, k14, yfwd,
k2 tog, k 53 (57) sts.
18th, 19th and 20th rows: work in st.st.
21st row: k 52 (56) sts, yfwd, k2 tog, k18, yfwd,
k2 tog, k 51 (55) sts.
22nd, 23rd and 24th rows: work in st.st.
25th row: k 50 (54) sts, yfwd, k2 tog, k22, yfwd,
k2 tog, k 49 (53) sts.
26th to 48th rows: work backwards from the
24th to the 2nd row inclusive.

Then work the 1st row once more. This completes the 3rd part of the pattern. Work 4 rows in st.st. This completes the 3 parts of the pattern.

Shape armhole and neck

With wrong side facing

1st row: k10, p 52 (56) sts, k1, p 52 (56) sts, k10.

2nd and following alternate rows: k.

tog, k4.

Repeat these last 2 rows 13 more times.

Shape neck

1st row: with wrong side facing, k4, p to last 4 sts, k4.

2nd row: k to last 6 sts, k2 tog, k4.

Repeat these last 2 rows 9 more times. (14: 18) sts. This completes the neck and armhole

3rd row: k11, p 50 (54) sts, k3, p 50 (54) sts, k11.

5th row: k12, p 48 (52) sts, k5, p 48 (52) sts, k12.

7th row: k13, p 46 (50) sts, k7, p 46 (50) sts, k13.

9th row: k14, p 44 (48) sts, k9, p 44 (48) sts, k14.

11th row: cast off 10 sts, k4, p 44 (48) sts, k9, p 44 (48) sts, k4, cast off last 10 sts. (105, 113) sts. Rejoin yarn.

next row: k 51 (55) sts, k2 tog, turn, leave remaining 52 (56) sts on a s.st.h and continue on these sts as follows:

1st row: k4, p to last 4 sts, k4.

2nd row: k4, sl.1, k1, psso, k to last 6 sts, k2

shaping. Continue straight for shoulder:

1st row: k4, p to last 4 sts, k4.

2nd row: k.

Repeat these last 2 rows until 31 (35) rows in all have been worked straight.

Shape back neck

1st row: with right side facing k to last 4 sts, inc into next st, k3.

2nd row: k2, inc into next st, p to last 4 sts, k4.

Repeat these last 2 rows 6 more times. (28: 32) sts.

next row: k.

Now leave these sts on a s.st.h and work other side to correspond reversing shaping as follows:
Pick up the 52 (56) sts on s.st.h, rejoin yarn and k to end of row.

Shape armhole and neck
1st row: k4, p to last 4 sts, k4.
2nd row: k4, sl.1, k1, psso, k to last 6 sts, k2 tog, k4.

Shape neck
1st row: k4, p to last 4 sts, k4.
2nd row: k4, sl.1, k1, psso, k to end of row.

Shape back neck
1st row: k2, inc into next st, k to end of row.
2nd row: k4, p to last 3 sts, inc knitwise into next st, k2.

Join shoulders and work back neck edge
With wrong side facing
next row: k4, p to last 4 sts, k4.
Now continuing on same row, cast on 21 sts, now continue on to sts on s.st.h, k4, p to last 4 sts, k4. (77: 85) sts.
next row: k.
1st row: k4, p 20 (24) sts, k 29, p 20 (24) sts, k4.
2nd and following alternate rows: k.
3rd row: k4, p 21 (25) sts, k 27, p 21 (25) sts, k4.
5th row: k4, p 22 (26) sts, k 25, p 22 (26) sts, k4.
7th row: k4, p 23 (27) sts, k 23, p 23 (27) sts, k4.
9th row: k4, p 24 (28) sts, k 21, p 24 (28) sts, k4.
This completes the back neck. Now work straight as follows:
1st row: k.
2nd row: k4, p to last 4 sts, k4.
Repeat these last 2 rows until 24 (28) rows have been worked straight and back corresponds to front length.

Shape armholes
With right side facing
1st row: k2, inc into next st, k to last 4 sts, inc into next st, k3.
2nd row: k4, p to last 4 sts, k4.
Repeat these last 2 rows until there are 103 (111) sts. Repeat 1st row once more. (105: 113) sts.
next row: cast on 10 sts, k4, p4 to last 4 sts, k4, cast on 10 sts. (125: 133) sts.
1st and following alternate rows: k.
2nd row: k14, p to last 14 sts, k14.
4th row: k13, p to last 13 sts, k13.
6th row: k12, p to last 12 sts, k12.
8th row: k11, p to last 11 sts, k11.
10th row: k10, p to last 10 sts, k10.
Now work straight in st.st until back corresponds to front length. Dec 1 st at the end of the last row. (124: 132) sts. Change to 2¼ mm (13) needles and work 8 cm (3 in) in k2, p2 rib. Cast off in rib.

MAKING UP
Work in all ends, sew side seams.

DANNY
Man's sweater in thick cotton

A summer sweater with twisted rib tramlines leading to an important centre cable. The body is in reverse stocking stitch and the collar in garter stitch set on a ribbed stand neck. Worn with white flannels, this is a terrific match for the sporty or spectator.

MATERIALS
15 (16: 17) 50 gm balls thick-weight cotton
2 3 mm (11) needles
2 3¾ mm (9) needles
4 3 mm (11) double pointed needles
cable needle
stitch holders

MEASUREMENTS
Chest
97 (102: 107: 112) cm
38 (40: 42: 44) in
Measurement at widest point
112 (117: 122: 127) cm
44 (46: 48: 50) in
Finished length to shoulder
68 (69: 70: 71) cm
26½ (27: 27½: 28) in
Sleeve length
59 (60: 61: 61) cm
23 (23½: 24: 24) in

TENSION
26 sts and 33 rows for a 10 cm (4 in) square worked in pattern on 3¾ mm (9) needles

BACK
* With 3mm (11) needles cast on 110 (116: 122: 128) sts. Work 9 cm (3½ in) in k2, p2 twisted rib (k into back of k st). Change to 3¾ mm (9) needles.
next row: with right side facing k 4 (7: 10: 13) sts, *k2, inc into next st; repeat from * to last 4 (7: 10: 13) sts, k to end of row. (144: 150: 156: 162) sts. Work 1 row in p. Now continue in pattern as follows:

1st row: with right side facing p 1 (4: 7: 1) sts, (kb1, p8) 5 (5: 5: 6) times, kb1, p4, rib next 11 sts thus:
(kb1, p1, to last st, kb1), p4, k12, p4, rib next 11 sts thus:
(kb1, p1, to last st, kb1), p4, (kb1, p8) 5 (5: 5: 6) times, kb1, p to end of row.
2nd row: k1 (4: 7: 1) sts, (pb1, k8) 5 (5: 5: 6) times, pb1, k4, rib next 11 sts thus:
(pb1, k1, to last st, pb1), k4, p12, k4, rib next 11 sts thus:
(pb1, k1, to last st, pb1), k4, (pb1, k8) 5 (5: 5: 6) times, pb1, k to end of row.
These 2 rows set the pattern. Work these 2 rows 10 more times.
23rd row: p 1 (4: 7: 1) sts, (kb1, p8) 5 (5: 5: 6) times, kb1, p4, rib next 11 sts as set, p4, cable next 12 sts thus:
put 1st 6 sts on a cable needle and leave at front of work, k6, k6 sts from cable needle, p4, rib 11 sts as set, p4, (kb1, p8) 5 (5: 5: 6) times, kb1, p to end of row.
These last 22 rows (2nd to 23rd inclusive) make the pattern. Continue repeating throughout until work measures 42 cm (16½ in) from cast on edge.
Shape armholes
With right side facing work the first 8 sts and put them on a s.st.h, work to the last 8 sts and put these on a s.st.h. Turn and continue on remaining 128 (134: 140: 146) sts.* Work straight for 85 (89: 93: 97) rows. Leave all sts on a s.st.h for shoulder seams and neck edge.

FRONT
Work the same as Back from * to *. Work straight for 55 (59: 63: 67) rows.

Shape neck

With right side facing work 52 (54: 56: 58) sts, turn and continue on these sts, keeping continuity of pattern correct dec 1 st at neck edge every row until 43 (45: 47: 49) sts remain. Work 20 rows to complete front to back

work facing each other. Then working on the right side of work, k tog a st from each needle to give 1 st on right hand needle. *K tog the next 2 sts (now 2 sts on right hand needle) then pass the 1st of these 2 sts over the 2nd. Repeat from * to work the rest of the sts.

finished length. Leave sts on a s.st.h for shoulder seam, leave centre 24 (26: 28: 30) sts on a s.st.h for neck edge, rejoin yarn to remaining 52 (54: 56: 58) sts and work to match other side.

Shoulder seam

Work 2 the same. With 3¾ mm (9) needles put 43 (45: 47: 49) sts from the back and the same from the front on to spare needles. Place these 2 needles side by side with the wrong sides of

Neck edge and collar

With right side facing and 4 3 mm (11) double pointed needles, start at centre front. Pick up and k 12 (13: 14: 15) sts from s.st.h (half of the neck edge), 23 sts up side front, 1 st at shoulder seam, 42 (44: 46: 48) sts from s.st.h (back neck edge), 1 st at shoulder seam, 23 sts down side front and remaining 12 (13: 14: 15) sts on s.st.h. (114: 118: 122: 126) sts. Work 8 rounds in k1, p1 twisted rib. Now divide for collar. At centre

front, turn and now working in rows, work 8 cm (3 in) in g.st (every row k). Cast off from *under* side of collar.

SLEEVES

Work 2 the same. With right side of work facing and 3¾ mm (9) needles, pick up and k 8 sts from s.st.h (armhole shaping), 125 (131: 137: 143) sts evenly along armhole edge with centre st at shoulder seam and 8 sts from s.st.h. (141: 147: 153: 159) sts. Now work in pattern as follows at the same time dec 1 st at each end of every 4th row.

1st row: with wrong side facing k 7 (1: 4: 7) sts, (pb1, k8) 14 (16: 16: 16) times, pb1, k to end of row.

2nd row: p 7 (1: 4: 7) sts, (kb1, p8) 14 (16: 16: 16) times, kb1, p to end of row.
These 2 rows set the pattern. Continue repeating throughout keeping continuity correct over dec until 61 (65: 69: 75) sts remain.

Shape cuff
With wrong side facing dec 7 (9: 11: 15) sts evenly across row. (54: 56: 58: 60) sts. Change to 3 mm (11) needles. Work 9 cm (3½ in) in k2, p2 twisted rib. Cast off *loosely* in rib.

MAKING UP

Work in all ends, sew throughout sleeve and side seams from cuff to welt. Sew a neat strengthening stitch to inside of neck edge where collar divides.

ACKNOWLEDGEMENTS

FOR MARION FOALE

Photography
Rick Best

Prints
Richard Duncan at Gordon Bishop Associates

Stylist
Marylyn Larkin

Extra clothing
Margaret Howell, Marion Foale, Jasper Conran and Cerruti

Hair
Gianni and Sally Francomb

Make up
Mark Easton and Candice Lauren

Premier Model Agency
Carole, Suzanne and Vicky

Models
Audrey Tom; Suzi Bick; Rejina; Richenda; Suzanne de Beck; Wendy Chayko; Estelle; Alice Gee; Brodie; John Pearson; Polly; Charley; Luke; Lucy; Rhona

Knitting Coordinator
Wendy Donahoe

Captions
Marit Allen

Planning and Organization
Chris Jones

FOR EDDISON/SADD

Design Director
Nick Eddison

Editorial Director
Ian Jackson

Pattern Checker
Anne Matthews

Proof Readers
Angela Jeffs and Charlotte Edwards

Designer
Clare Clements

Production
Bob Towell